THE FLY FISHERMAN'S

ENTOMOLOGICAL PATTERN BOOK

JOHN CAWTHORNE

The Crowood Press

First published in 2000 by
The Crowood Press Ltd
Ramsbury, Marlborough
Wiltshire SN8 2HR

© John Cawthorne 2000

**British Library Cataloguing-in-
Publication Data**

A catalogue record for this book is available
from the British Library.

ISBN 1 86126 320 1

To
Margaret and Tom Richardson,
who will always be as much
a part of Monsal Dale as the river itself.

For
Anne, Mavis, William and Kelly

Many thanks to
Carol, Jack Shardlow, Tom Richardson
and Wilf Skelton

Designed and edited by Focus Publishing,
Sevenoaks, Kent

Printed and bound in China

Acknowledgements

Any talent I have for fly fishing has been the
result, to a great extent, of the people who
have influenced me through my fishing years.
My collection of books, for I not only love fly
fishing but also have a passion for reading
about it, contains volumes by some of the
great writers and fishermen both past and
present. Skues, Halford, Courtney Williams,
Ronalds, Sawyer, John Roberts, Goddard
and Clarke, Taff Price, Charles Jardine, to
name but a few. But there is another great
hero of mine from this pleasure of fly fishing
who is perhaps the father of it all. His name
was G. S. Marryat.

We all, on our own rivers, have men who,
like Marryat, will perhaps never write books
or seek fame but who, nevertheless,
influence us greatly in our fly fishing. The
following are my 'Marryats'– three river-
keepers and two very fine fly fishermen. First
was David Hunt, the keeper on the Bolton
Priory stretch of the River Wharfe. Second,
Jack Shardlow, my initial teacher in the art of
fly fishing, to whom I owe so much. Jack and
I fished the Wharf and our local river, the
Don, and this was more than ably looked
after by the voluntary river keeper, Peter
Towers, and his small band of helpers. They
transformed the river, with a lot of hard work,
into a delightful small river fishery. I then took
a rod on the River Wye at Monsal Dale in
Derbyshire. The river keeper, Tom
Richardson, has looked after the stretch for
many years and it must rank as one of the
finest fisheries in the country.

My fishing partner of the past five seasons
has been Wilf Skelton. Both Tom and Wilf
have taught me many things about fishing
and their company is as enjoyable as the
fishing. Together Wilf and I have collected
specimens, compared flies and spent many
hours observing and filming the goings-on
on the river. Without the influence and
encouragement of these men this book
would never have been completed.
I thank them all.

Contents

Introduction

This book is mainly about the art of Impressionism, for just like the group of artists striving to portray movement, form, colour and the effect of light on a flat surface, so the fly designer faces the same challenges but in 3-dimensional form. Apart from the actual movement of the fly and nymph being controlled by the fisherman's actions so the tying of the fly itself is done in such a way as to effect an impression of movement in the artificial. An exact copy of the natural fly is not only unattainable, but undesirable. Any natural fly, in or on the water, will show some signs of movement; at times the movement is the trigger to the trout's reactions. We have all been educated to the use of the induced take where a nymph of fairly basic design is drifted down towards the fish and a slight movement of the rod at the correct moment will make the nymph rise in the water and induce the trout to take it. This is a movement totally controlled and created by the angler, but subtler movements can be built into both nymph and fly by the flytier.

The natural fly has six legs but in order to create a sense of movement in the artificial we put into the design an excess of legs which, especially when coupled with water surface movements, effects of air flow,and so on, give an impression of life to the fly. The same feather fibres that we use to create an impression of legs beneath the fly can also be used to imitate the presence of wings above the fly. The natural wing is so very fine that the fibres represent the veins and the light acting upon the facets of the wing. The use of feather slips as wings, although excellent to represent the overall shape, are mostly far too dense to imitate the gossamer fineness of the natural wing. The portrayal of a denser form of wing is more useful in the patterns of sedges, stoneflies and other miscellaneous flies and indeed some excellent materials are available for this purpose.

Tails are mostly imitated by the use of feather fibres or newer materials such as microfibetts, both of which give an appearance of life and movement. Although some anglers and flytiers regard tails as of no importance it does seem rather pointless to omit them from the artificial when they are present in the natural.

The body of the nymph and dry fly can be made from many different materials depending on the effect desired. Legs and gills giving movement in the natural nymph must also be echoed in the artificial. This can be achieved by the use of various dubbing materials, feather herls, fur and synthetics. These can then be underweighted or covered with p.v.c. or similar material to create a segmented body whilst leaving some fibres protruding to act as gills, legs and so on. The body of the dry fly can be made with similar materials but remembering that we need it to float, the use of buoyant materials, such as deer hair, waxed thread, stripped hackle stalk, various suitable dubbing materials and so on, come into their own.

The form of the nymph can be achieved more easily than that of the dry fly. Nymphs, for the most part, have a tapering abdomen and a bulkier area in the thorax and wing-cases. There are variations to this basic shape but mostly of a minor nature, stone-clingers are broad and flattened, agile-darters are as you would expect, more streamlined. By studying the naturals the correct shape is fairly easy to execute and by the addition of weight in the form of lead wire we can fish them at the correct depth. The form of the dry fly is more complex and there are many variations of style – some dry flies have upright wings, some tent-shaped, some flat.

Upright wings are represented with feather slips, cut wings, hackle fibres, polypropylene yarn and so on. Tent-shaped wings can be created with feather slips, deer hair, curtain material or other synthetics like Roman Moser wings. Flat wings can be made from similar materials. Although the materials do matter, the finished shape and how to achieve it is the important consideration and this can be done with a variety of different materials.

The body form of the fly is usually slim and segmented but we do not always adhere to this principle for we have to consider the effect of light and colour. Many of the naturals are translucent and subject to transmitted and reflected light, reflected light coming from its surroundings and the transmitted light from the natural itself. The reflected light will alter the colour of the natural – to some extent this can be overcome by the addition of translucent materials in the tying. Also dubbed bodies are used to a larger extent than solid bodies. We also have other outside factors acting upon the design of the fly. A fly or nymph seen against a bright sky will be more of a silhouette whereas a fly seen in shade will show its colours more clearly. The view of the trout is another factor to be taken into consideration – the effect of objects seen in the 'mirror' and the 'window' of the trout's world.

The overriding factor is to stay true to size, form, texture, colour and so on. It then follows that the outside effects of background, lighting, the trout's view will be as similar as possible on the artificial as on the natural. All the patterns shown in the book have been designed by their originators on that premise.

If you count up the number of patterns included in this book, and there are of course many more available that are not included, you would need to carry a suitcase and a catalogue with you on your fishing trips. You can, of course, narrow the selection down by having a sound working knowledge of your own particular fishing situations. This can be achieved to some extent by the use of a few basic 'tools' and some of your valuable fishing time. Flies and nymphs can be collected by the use of a small net and specimen tubes. Another very useful item is a small hand lens. Flies not normally found in your area can then be eliminated from the artificials in your fly box. There is another side to this – the more anglers become involved in the gathering of this information, the more knowledge will be available to anglers and entomologists everywhere. There is still a great amount of information to be gathered regarding the entomology of rivers and lakes, distribution, hatching times and so on, in which there are still a lot of 'grey' areas.

Most anglers of course haven't the time for this taxing occupation and so the list of artificials has to be reduced by other methods. A selection of dry flies and nymphs have to be arrived at by some other means. If, for instance, a fly is regarded as belonging to chalkstreams or lowland waters, then the northern fisherman can eliminate it from his required list and, indeed, a number of flies can be eliminated in this way. Flies have months of emergence. Early season flies, for instance, can be carried at the time they are likely to be required but left out of the fly box when not. Two of the most obvious examples of this are the Hawthorn fly, a very early season fly for a short period only, and the fisherman's favourite, the Mayfly, that is relevant for a maximum of two to three weeks.

Even if this kind of selection is too much trouble then a choice of general impressionistic flies is the answer. For instance, the Grey Duster in a variety of sizes will catch fish throughout the season. This fly, together with a Gold Ribbed Hare's Ear nymph, also in various sizes, would give you reasonably good fishing throughout the season on almost any water. But of course a lot of the joy of trying to outwit the fish with a reasonable copy of the food it is taking is lost and also some of the art of fly fishing. Fishermen have gone to great pains to attempt the impossible and play Mother Nature at her own game by producing artificials so close to the naturals that a wild creature with all its sense for survival is deceived and this is the art and the pleasure of fly fishing.

1 Mayfly

(Ephemera Danica, Vulgata, Lineata)

Of these three species of mayfly only *E. Danica* and *E. Vulgata* are of any significance to the angler in Britain, *E. Lineata* being somewhat of a rarity.

The life cycle consists of four stages and starts with the fertilized female flying over the water and dipping her abdomen below the surface. Eggs fall to the bottom where they become attached to rocks, stones and weeds. After a period of development the young nymphs hatch out. They spend their time living and growing in small open-ended tunnels which they burrow into the sand and mud of the riverbed. The nymphs, which moult many times in their life, have an elongated body with three long tails. They feed on decaying plant material and algae that they scrape from the surface of stones with their very strong jaws. The male nymph is usually smaller than the female which may grow up to 35mm. They are very slow-moving but have the ability to take in water and eject it rapidly in order to propel themselves forward. It is only when they make their way to the surface to moult (after about two years) that they are free-swimming and also at their most vulnerable stage. At the surface the sub-imago or dun emerges. It is capable of flying immediately, although in wet weather it does take a longer time to get airborne and therefore is at greater risk of being taken by a trout. Once airborne the dun flies to some object near the water for the final moult into the true adult. The final stage being the imago (spinner) the mayfly has now a much brighter, more colourful appearance with very shiny wings.

Courting males may be seen dancing in huge swarms over the water. If a suitable female comes by, the male will grab her from below and mating takes place. Soon after mating the male will fall to the ground and die. The female will start egg-laying almost at once, flying low over the water and dipping her abdomen under the surface to release her eggs. When this task is complete she too will fall to the surface and die to provide food for hungry trout.

Size:	Nymph: up to 35mm. Adult: up to 30mm
Distribution:	Abundant in most parts of Britain but localized in Northern England and Scotland
Habitat:	*E. Danica* – fast flowing water *E. Vulgata* – slow flowing with muddy bed
Season:	May – June
Hatch:	Early afternoon – early evening
Description:	Nymph: Cream-coloured body with dark markings and three long tails
Sub-imago:	Mottled wings with brown markings, body greyish-white in male and creamy-yellow in female, three long tails
Imago:	Pale creamy body with sparkling, heavily veined, transparent wings. Hind wings much smaller than forewings, three long tails

Nymph and Emerger

1. Walkers Mayfly Nymph

Hook length: 25mm
Thread: Dark brown
Tail: Fibres from a pheasant's tail
Abdomen: Yellow-buff angora wool over lead underbody
Rib: Pheasant tail fibres
Thorax: Yellow-buff angora wool with fibres picked out
Wingcases: Pheasant tail fibres doubled with ends turned under for legs

2. Mayfly Nymph

Hook length: 25mm
Thread: Dark brown
Tail: Hare fibres
Abdomen: Cream Antron
Rib: Brown Floss
Thorax: Cream Antron picked out
Wingcases: Deer hair with ends turned under for legs

3. Suspender Mayfly Nymph

Hook length: 25mm
Thread: Dark brown
Tail: Cream Ostrich herl
Abdomen: White, yellow and tan seal's fur sub (2:1:1)
Rib: Dark brown thread
Thorax: As for abdomen picked out
Wingcases: In the place of wingcases a ball of ethaform in nylon mesh coloured brown

4. Mayfly Nymph

Hook length: 25mm
Thread: Dark brown
Tail: Fibres from a pheasant's tail
Abdomen: Cream and brown seal's fur sub (3:1) palmered with brown hackle
Rib: Dark brown thread
Thorax: As abdomen and picked out
Wingcases: Pheasant tail fibres doubled with ends turned down for legs

5. Emerger Mayfly Nymph

Hook length: 25mm
Thread: Dark brown
Tail: Pheasant tail fibres
Abdomen: Cream and brown rabbit's fur
Rib: Dark brown thread
Thorax: Pearlescent Spectraflash strands over abdomen fur picked out
Wing: Deer hair

6. Hatching Mayfly

Hook length: 25mm
Thread: Dark brown
Tail: Pheasant tail fibres
Abdomen: Pheasant tail fibres
Rib: Copper wire
Thorax: Yellow olive seal's fur sub
Wing: Roe deer hair with ginger hackle palmered length of thorax

Mayfly (Adult, Nymph)
(*Ephemera Danica, Vulgata, Lineata*)

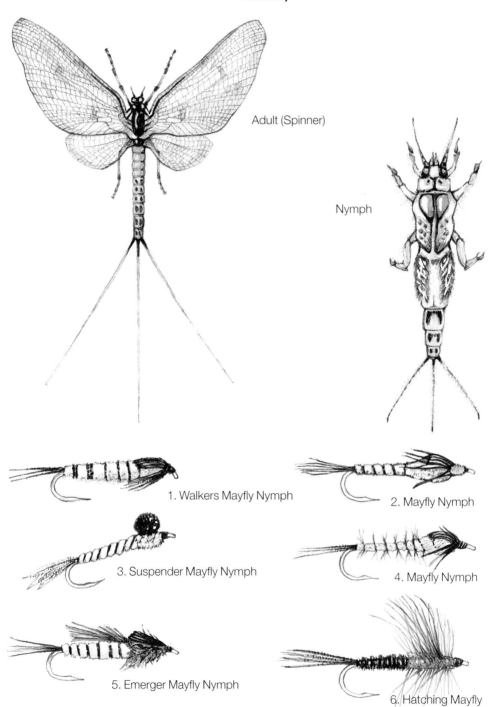

Adult (Spinner)

Nymph

1. Walkers Mayfly Nymph

2. Mayfly Nymph

3. Suspender Mayfly Nymph

4. Mayfly Nymph

5. Emerger Mayfly Nymph

6. Hatching Mayfly

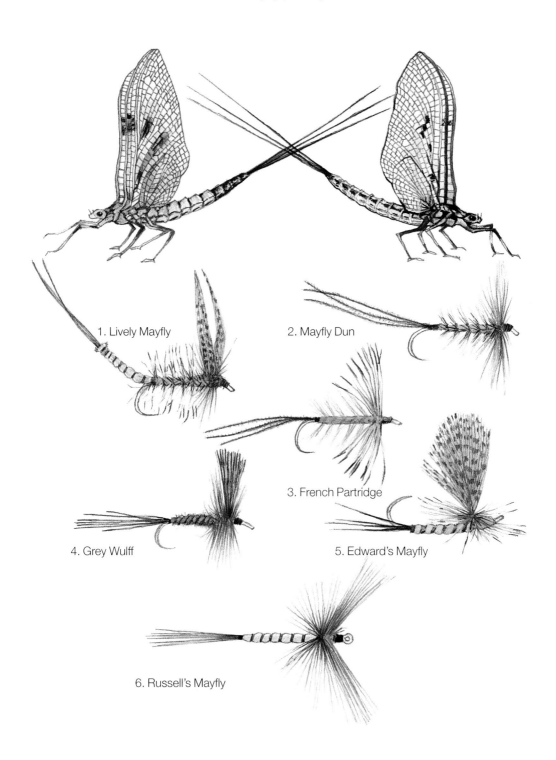

1. Lively Mayfly

2. Mayfly Dun

3. French Partridge

4. Grey Wulff

5. Edward's Mayfly

6. Russell's Mayfly

1. Lively Mayfly

DRESSING

Hook length: 20–25mm
Thread: Green
Tail: Three fibres from a pheasant tail
Abdomen: This is extended by the use of deer hair
Rib: Green thread
Thorax: Cream-yellow poly dubbing
Wing: Wood duck fibres separated into two bunches
Hackles: Body Grizzle cock
Head: Golden-olive cock

2. Mayfly Dun

DRESSING

Hook length: 20–25mm
Thread: Claret
Tail: Three pheasant tail fibres
Abdomen: Raffia
Hackles: Body: Palmered Badger cock
Head: Light olive cock

3. French Partridge Mayfly

DRESSING

Hook length: 20–25mm
Thread: Dark brown
Tail: Three pheasant tail fibres
Abdomen: Raffia
Rib: Gold wire
Hackles: Body: Palmered olive cock
Head: French Partridge feather

4. Grey Wulff

DRESSING

Hook length: 20–25mm
Thread: Black
Tail: Brown calf tail or deer hair
Abdomen: Grey rabbit fur
Wing: Brown calf or deer hair to form two bunches
Hackle: Blue dun cock

5. Edward's Mayfly

DRESSING

Hook length: 20–25mm (Swedish Dry fly hook)
Tail: Moose mane or deer hair
Abdomen: Mixed ivory seal's fur sub and ivory poly dubbing over silver lurex
Rib: Brown rayon or nylon floss
Thorax: Ivory and brown poly dubbing
Wing: Silver mallard breast or flank feather dyed pale yellow or lemon wood duck
Hackles: Pale blue dun, grizzle dyed lemon-yellow, tied parachute

6. Russell's Mayfly

DRESSING

Hook length: 20–25mm
Thread: Black
Tail: Brown cock fibres
Abdomen: Strip of polyethylene foam
Rib: Natural red cock hackle stalk
Wing: Dyed slate-blue cock hackle fibres in two bunches tied slanting forward either side of the eye
Hackle: Badger cock

2 Alderfly

(Sialis Lutaria, Sialis Fuliginosa)

We can consider both these species of alderfly together. *Sialis Lutaria* is much the commonest. During May and June they can be found in large numbers on waterside vegetation, they are not strong fliers and spend much of their time resting and crawling on plants and stones at the water's edge.

After mating the female lays her cigar-shaped eggs in batches on the underside of overhanging vegetation. Upon hatching the larvae fall to the riverbed to live in the silt and mud on the bottom. Alderfly larvae, with their stout, brownish bodies, are among the commonest of freshwater animals. They lead an active, predatory life feeding on a wide range of smaller insects including caddis and mayfly nymphs. The larvae spends about a year in the water before reaching its full size. In spring, it crawls out onto the bank and digs a small hole in soft, damp soil in which to pupate. After two or three weeks the final moult takes place and the adult fly emerges.

The wings take a short time to expand and dry before the adult fly can take to the air.

Size:	Larva: up to 40mm
	Adult: 10–16mm
Distribution:	Common and widely distributed
Habitat:	Margins of ponds, lakes and rivers
Season:	May – Mid–June
Hatch:	Daytime
Description:	Larva: Single-tailed about 40mm long. Stout, brownish body with distinct yellow markings. Large, powerful jaws
Adult:	Dark, soft-bodied fly with head and legs almost black. The four hard, shiny wings are heavily veined and held roof-shaped when at rest. Long jointed antennae

(Larvae and Adult)

1. Ombudsman

Hook length: 25mm
Thread: Brown
Abdomen: Bronze peacock herl
Rib: Copper wire
Wing: Dark, mottled hen wing feather tied flat over abdomen
Hackle: Brown hen

2. Alder Larva

Hook length: 25mm
Thread: Dark brown
Tail: White marabou
Abdomen: Hare's ear and rust Antron, the white marabou is left showing as a strip down each side
Rib: Gold wire
Thorax: Brown-olive seal's fur sub
Hackle: Brown partridge doubled over thorax with tips left for legs

3. Alder Larva

Hook length: 25mm
Thread: Dark brown
Tail: Brown cock fibres
Abdomen: Chestnut-brown seal's fur sub
Rib: Oval gold
Thorax: Brown seal's fur sub picked out
Hackle: Ginger tied behind thorax
Thorax and Abdomen cover: Brown fibres

4. Alder

Hook length: 15mm
Thread: Black
Abdomen: Magenta peacock herl
Wing: Brown hen
Hackle: Black cock

5. Herefordshire Alder

Hook length: 15mm
Thread: Yellow
Abdomen: Cock pheasant centre tail feather fibres
Hackle: Medium blue-dun cock

Alderfly (Adult, eggs, larva, pupa) (*Sialis lutaria*, *Fuliginosa*)

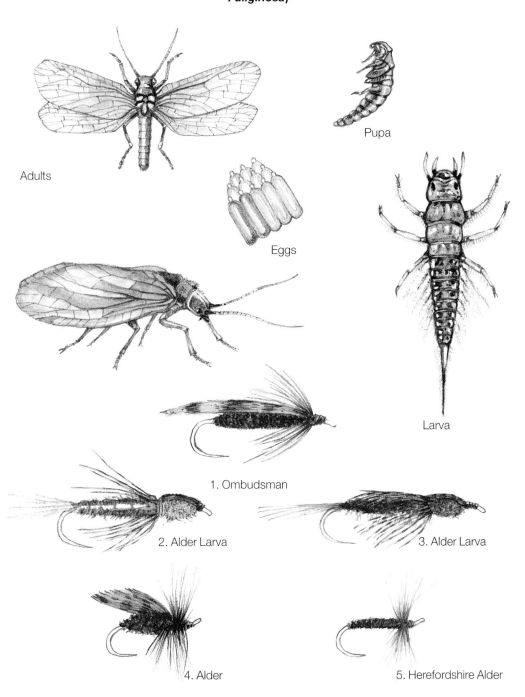

Pupa

Adults

Eggs

Larva

1. Ombudsman

2. Alder Larva

3. Alder Larva

4. Alder

5. Herefordshire Alder

3 Midges

(Chironomidae)

With over four hundred species of *chironomids* in Britain they are common everywhere and live near any type of water. They may even be found in stagnant and polluted waters due to their ability to live where there is a low oxygen content. Being present in such large numbers they are an important source of food for fish, especially in their larval and pupal stages.

Egg masses that are laid at the water surface are in long spiral ropes protected by a mass of jelly and are attached to plants and submerged stones. The tiny larvae that hatch out provide a good source of food for hungry trout. Midge larvae are commonly referred to as 'bloodworms', although not all of them are red. The red colour is due to the presence of haemoglobin in the blood and it is this that enables them to survive in a low oxygen presence. These worm-like creatures may grow up to 30mm long.

When the larva has changed into its pupal form it remains at the bottom for several days before floating up to the surface. The pupae, which have the ability to swim and may be of various colours, hang in the surface film for several minutes before the adults emerge.

During this time they again fall prey to hungry fish.

Towards dusk huge swarms of male midges may be seen hovering about in their mating dance in the hope of attracting suitable females. As these midges go through more than one life cycle in the year, hatches occur throughout the fishing season.

Size:	Larva: Various
	Adult: Various
Distribution:	Widespread and very abundant
Habitat:	All water types
Hatch:	Late afternoon and evening
Season:	All year
Description:	Larva: Wormlike body – various colours.
	Pupa: Slender, segmented body with white plumes on head and tail – various colours
	Adult: Cylindrical body with humped thorax and long legs. Transparent wings lying flat over the body. Male has feathery antennae

1. Bloodworm

Hook length: 7–15mm
Thread: Red
Tail: Feather fibres dyed red
Abdomen: Feather fibres dyed red
Rib: Oval silver tinsel
Thorax: Brown heron herl

2. Bloodworm

Hook length: 7–15mm (sedge hook)
Thread: Red
Tail: Red marabou
Abdomen: Red floss varnished
Thorax: Dubbed red and olive seal's
fur sub over lead underbody

3. Bloodworm

Hook length: 7–15mm (sedge hook)
Thread: Red
Abdomen: Red tinsel under with ribbing
of red lurex
Thorax: Red lurex over underbody of lead

4. Suspender Midge Pupa

Hook length: 15mm
Thread: Brown
Abdomen: Seal's fur sub various colours
Rib: Fine silver wire
Thorax: Peacock herl
Suspender: Ethafoam ball enclosed in fine
nylon mesh (ladies tights)

5. Phantom Larva

Hook length: 15mm
Abdomen: Grey, fluorescent floss wound from
hook eye to half way round bend, two air
bladders marked with indelible black felt-tip,
then covered with clear varnish

6. Phantom Larva

Hook length: 15mm
Abdomen: White fluorescent floss
p.v.c. covered
Rib: Fine silver wire
Thorax: Very fine bronze dubbing

7. Midge Pupa

DRESSING

Hook length: 15mm (sedge hook)
Abdomen: Marabou floss silk
in various colours
Rib: Fine copper wire
Thorax: Seal's fur sub to match abdomen

8. Midge Pupa

DRESSING

Hook length: 15mm (sedge hook)
Abdomen: Floss silk to match
Rib: Silver wire
Thorax: Peacock herl or to match
seal's fur sub
Breathing filaments: Fluorescent white wool

9. Hatching Midge Pupa

DRESSING

Hook length: 15mm
Thread: Red or colour to match
Abdomen: Marabou silk to match
Rib: Silver lurex. Abdomen and rib covered
with p.v.c.
Thorax: To match turkey herl or peacock
Breathing filaments: White fluorescent wool

10. Midge

DRESSING

Hook length: 5–12mm
Thread: Brown silk
Abdomen: Brown or black silk
Wing: Two white hackle points tied over back
Hackle: Grizzle cock

11. Knotted Midge

DRESSING

Hook length: 5–12mm
Thread: Black
Abdomen: Black thread
Hackle: Two black cock at either end of
abdomen

12. Halford's Black Gnat

DRESSING

Hook length: 5–12mm
Thread: Black
Abdomen: Black thread
Wing: Grey Mallard tied sloping backwards
Hackle: Black cock

Midges (Larvae, pupae, adult) (*Chironomidae*)

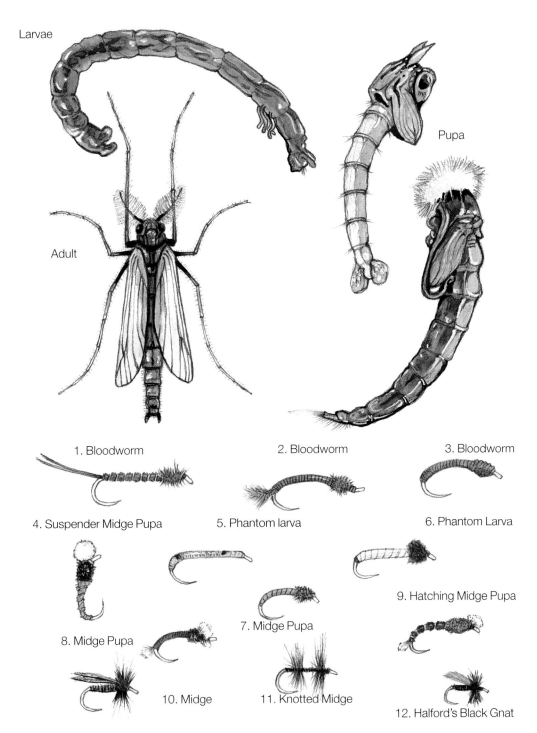

Larvae

Pupa

Adult

1. Bloodworm

2. Bloodworm

3. Bloodworm

4. Suspender Midge Pupa

5. Phantom larva

6. Phantom Larva

9. Hatching Midge Pupa

7. Midge Pupa

8. Midge Pupa

10. Midge

11. Knotted Midge

12. Halford's Black Gnat

4 Great Red Sedge

(Phryganea Grandis, Phryganea Striata)

Having a wide distribution and being found in many large rivers and lakes these are the only two common sedge to inhabit still or slow-flowing sections of water. They are amongst the largest of British sedges, being from 20–27mm long, the female usually slightly larger than the male.

Eggs are deposited on surface vegetation in gelatinous ropes. Upon hatching the larva falls into the water and spins a silk sheath around its abdomen to which it attaches small sections of plant material. These sections are cut to shape and cemented together in a characteristic spiral pattern forming a cylinder which twists to the left. Larvae may be up to 40mm long, the case being slightly larger. *Phryganea* lives as a larva for about a year before going through its pupal phase. The adult flies emerge mostly during late evening in open water and then make their way to land. In Ireland, where this sedge is an important fly, it is known as the Murragh.

Size:	Larva: up to 50mm.
	Adult: 20-27mm
Distribution:	Widely distributed in lakes and rivers
Habitat:	Still or slow flowing water
Season:	Late May/June/July
Hatch:	Mostly late evening
Description:	Larva: Pale bodied with bright yellow head with two dark bands, case of plant material
	Adult: Grey-brown body with broad reddish-brown wings with paler areas

Sedges

1. Cased Caddis

DRESSING

Hook length: 30mm
Thread: Black
Abdomen: Hare's ear over lead underbody
Thorax: White swan or goose herl
Hackle: Black hen to represent legs
Head: Black thread tied bulky and varnished

2. Cased Caddis

DRESSING

Hook length: 30mm
Thread: Dark brown
Abdomen: Golden pheasant centre tail fibres over lead
Rib: Gold wire
Thorax: Hare's ear fur
Hackle: Brown partridge to represent legs
Head: Peacock herl

Great Red Sedge (Adult, larva, pupa)
(*Phryganea grandis, striata*)

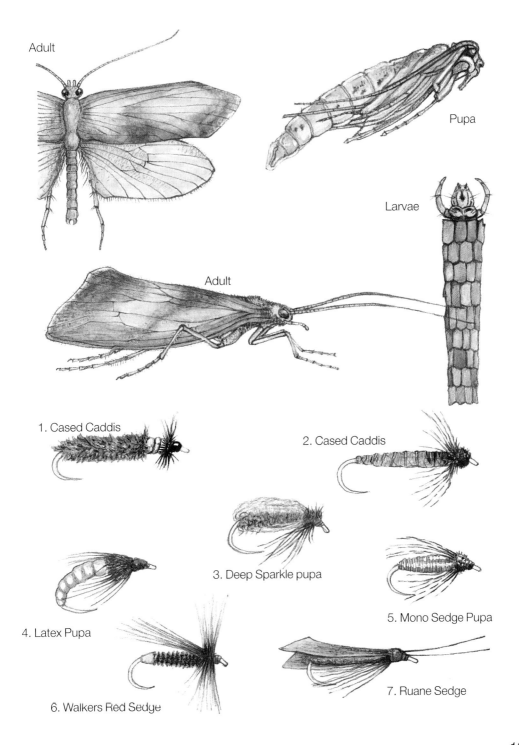

Adult

Pupa

Larvae

Adult

1. Cased Caddis

2. Cased Caddis

3. Deep Sparkle pupa

4. Latex Pupa

5. Mono Sedge Pupa

6. Walkers Red Sedge

7. Ruane Sedge

3. Deep Sparkle Pupa

DRESSING

Hook length: 20mm
Thread: Orange
Abdomen: Sparkle yarn with natural fur colours to suit over a copper wire body. Outer body of sparkle yarn tied in front and rear to represent the gas build-up in natural
Thorax: Marabou herl orange
Hackle: Partridge fibres to represent emerging legs

4. Latex Pupa

DRESSING

Hook length: 20mm
Thread: Brown
Abdomen: Fluorescent lime-green floss
Rib: Cream-coloured latex
Thorax: Brown ostrich herl
Hackle: Brown hen

5. Mono Sedge Pupa

DRESSING

Hook length: 20mm
Thread: Brown or white
Abdomen: Built up of tying thread
Rib: Nylon monofilament covering the abdomen and built up towards thorax
Thorax: Peacock herl
Hackle: Partridge

6. Walker Red Sedge

DRESSING

Hook length: 20mm
Thread: Tan
Abdomen: Tip of abdomen arc–chrome wool to represent egg sac of natural female, rest – brown ostrich herl or pheasant tail
Wing: Red cock fibres
Hackle: Long-fibred red cock

7. Ruane Sedge

DRESSING

Hook length: 20mm
Thread: Green
Abdomen: Insect-green poly dubbing
Wing: Brown Fly-Rite Poly II cut to shape
Hackle: Green deer hair tied under the body to represent legs
Antennae: Hackle stalks

5 Sedge or Caddis Fly

More than two hundred species of Sedge Fly live in the British Isles and can be found in any type of water. Adult flies are active mostly at dusk, spending the day hiding in vegetation, although a few daytime flying species do exist.

Sedge Flies have four wings that when at rest lie folded along the body in the shape of a ridged roof. These wings have a covering of very fine hairs, distinguishing them from moths to which they bear a close resemblance. The position of the wings at rest also distinguishes them from both Stoneflies (flatwinged) and Mayflies (upwinged). All Sedge Flies are tailless and have very long, many-jointed antennae, sometimes twice the length of the body.

The life cycle follows a standard egg, larva, pupa, adult pattern. Eggs are laid either on the water surface, under the water or on over-hanging vegetation depending on the species. Whichever method is followed the eggs fall to the bottom and the jelly-like covering they have swells up to protect them. Once the larvae hatch out they proceed to build protective cases around their bodies. Each species builds to a particular design using specific materials – grit, sand, twigs, plant materials and so on. The pieces that make up the casings are cemented together and, as the larva grows, new material is added.

Although the caddis case is open at both ends to allow a through flow of water, the rear end is often very narrow, whilst the front end is large enough for head and legs to protrude to allow movement.

Some species of sedge do not live in cases but spin silky nets that both afford some protection to the insect as well as acting as a food trap. Nearly all these net-making species live in running water and have tougher bodies than case-making flies. Some species of sedge are free-swimming and build neither a case nor a net.

When the larva is fully grown and ready for pupation, case-making caddis anchor one end to a firm object and seal both ends of the case. Net-making and free-living species build special pupal chambers from sand and spin a cocoon around themselves inside the chamber. Once fully formed the adult insect bites its way out of the larval case and swims to the surface. Although some pupae do swim ashore and climb onto vegetation, emergence usually takes place at the surface where they cause quite a disturbance in their efforts to get airborne. Newly emerged caddis often fly over the water in considerable numbers and draw the attention of hungry trout.

1. Rhyacophila larva

DRESSING

Hook length: 17mm
Thread: Brown
Tail: Brown feather fibres short
Abdomen: Olive Antron dubbed clear p.v.c. strip over back
Rib: Yellow mono or gold wire
Thorax/Head: Brown Antron dubbed
Legs: Mottled feather for legs and wingcases

2. Free-Swimming larva

DRESSING

Hook length: 17mm
Thread: Green or brown to match
Tail: Brown feather fibres short
Abdomen: Green or brown dubbing clear p.v.c. strip over back
Rib: Gold wire
Thorax: Green or brown dubbing
Legs: Short brown feather
Wingcases: Brown or green feather fibres over

(Larvae and Pupal Stages)

3. Rhyacophila pupa

DRESSING

Hook length: 17mm (Grub/Sedge hook)
Thread: Brown
Abdomen: Olive Antron or similar dubbing
Rib: Gold wire
Thorax: Brown dubbing
Hackle: Grouse

4. M.M.G. Cased Caddis

DRESSING

Hook length: 25mm
Thread: Black
Abdomen: Dubbed brown, grizzle hackle, brown seal fur sub twisted along hook and dipped to shape. Fibres left longer at head end.*
Rib: Gold wire
Thorax: See Abdomen
* Stripped hackle stalks can be tied in at the bend and eye of the hook to represent twigs stuck to some natural cases

5. Rackelhane

DRESSING

Hook length: 20mm
Thread: Dark brown
Abdomen: Olive seal's fur sub
Legs: Mix of yellow and brown hair

6. Green Stick

DRESSING

Hook length: 25mm
Thread: Green or black
Abdomen: Green floss silk. Green raffia over
Thorax: Green or yellow floss silk
Legs: Short ginger hen

7. Plant Cased Caddis

DRESSING

Hook length: 25mm
Thread: Brown
Abdomen: Dubbed brown hair fibres and clipped deer hair
Thorax: Dubbed yellow hare's ear, brown latex over
Legs: Short, black cock

8. Cased Caddis

DRESSING

Hook length: 25mm
Thread: Black
Abdomen: Dubbed golden pheasant tail fibres chopped short
Thorax: Green silk
Legs: Golden pheasant tail fibres

Caddis-Flies (Larvae and various cases)
(a, b, c are all non-case making species)

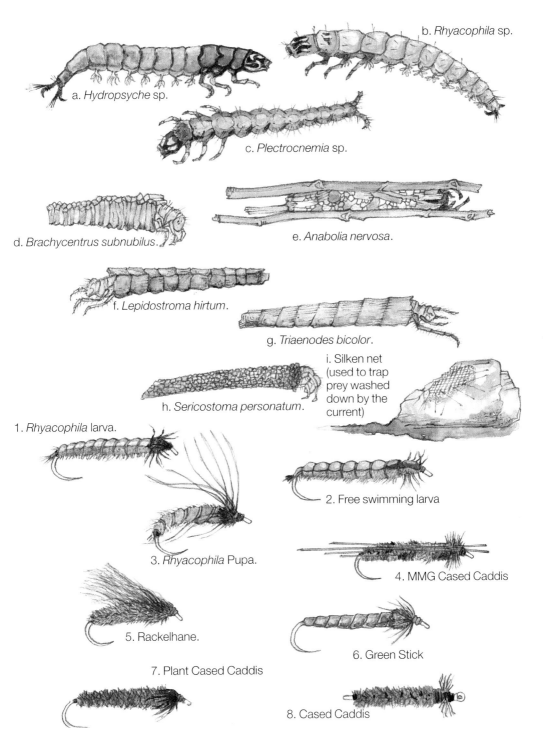

b. *Rhyacophila* sp.

a. *Hydropsyche* sp.

c. *Plectrocnemia* sp.

d. *Brachycentrus subnubilus*.

e. *Anabolia nervosa*.

f. *Lepidostroma hirtum*.

g. *Triaenodes bicolor*.

h. *Sericostoma personatum*.

i. Silken net (used to trap prey washed down by the current)

1. *Rhyacophila* larva.

2. Free swimming larva

3. *Rhyacophila* Pupa.

4. MMG Cased Caddis

5. Rackelhane.

6. Green Stick

7. Plant Cased Caddis

8. Cased Caddis

(Larvae and Pupae Stages)

1. Sand Caddis

Hook length: 20mm
Thread: Black or Brown
Abdomen: Green or cream floss covered in adhesive then covered with fine sand
Thorax: Fluorescent green floss
Legs: Brown partridge

2. Pebble Caddis

Hook length: 25mm
Thread: Black or brown
Abdomen: Green or cream floss covered in adhesive then covered with vermiculite
Thorax: Fluorescent green floss
Legs: Brown partridge

3. Pebble Cased Caddis

Hook length: 20mm
Thread: Brown
Abdomen: Grey-tan chenille
Thorax: Deer hair and brown fibres
Legs: As thorax picked out

4. Sedge Pupa

Hook length: 20mm (Sedge hook)
Thread: Yellow
Abdomen: Antron and seal's fur sub 50/50 in ginger colours
Rib: Clear polythene
Wingcases: Dyed white duck feathers to match abdomen, tied either side
Thorax: As abdomen but without the rib. Two bronze Mallard fibres tied in under thorax facing backwards
Legs: Dyed partridge to match body

5. Peeping Caddis

Hook length: 25mm
Thread: Brown
Abdomen: Hare's fur dubbed at the hook eye end, a single lead shot is tied in
Rib: Gold wire
Thorax: Light-coloured wool, tip of the wool burnt to form a black head
Legs: Partridge hackle

6. Hatching Sedge Pupa

Hook length: 10–18mm
Thread: Orange
Abdomen: Orange seal's fur sub
Rib: Gold wire
Thorax: Natural deer hair spun and clipped
Legs: Brown partridge, rear sloping under thorax

Caddis-Flies (Larvae and various cases)

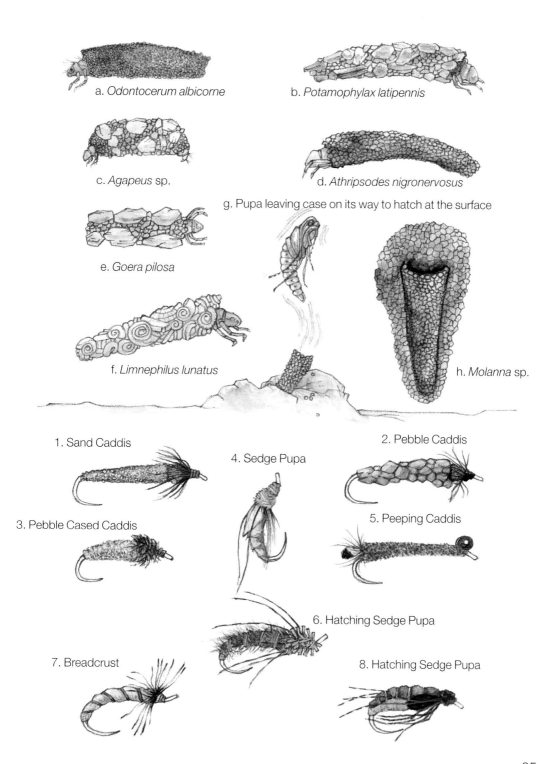

a. *Odontocerum albicorne*

b. *Potamophylax latipennis*

c. *Agapeus* sp.

d. *Athripsodes nigronervosus*

e. *Goera pilosa*

g. Pupa leaving case on its way to hatch at the surface

f. *Limnephilus lunatus*

h. *Molanna* sp.

1. Sand Caddis

2. Pebble Caddis

4. Sedge Pupa

3. Pebble Cased Caddis

5. Peeping Caddis

6. Hatching Sedge Pupa

7. Breadcrust

8. Hatching Sedge Pupa

7. Breadcrust

Hook length: 10–18mm (Sedge hook)
Thread: Orange
Abdomen: Orange floss
Rib: Stripped brown cock hackle quill
Legs: Soft grizzle hen hackle

8. Hatching Sedge Pupa

Hook length: 10–18mm (Sedge hook)
Thread: Green
Abdomen: Light green fly-rite poly dubbing covered over back with dark green dyed swan shoulder
Rib: Gold wire
Wingcases: Dark brown Raffene in two loops either side of thorax
Thorax: Sepia and brown seal's fur sub
Antennae: Wood duck fibres
Legs and Head: Cock pheasant tail fibres tied in and wound to form head

6 Sedges (Adult)

Yellow Spotted, Cinnamon, Grannom

Yellow Spotted (*Philoptamus Montanus*)

This sedge prefers faster flowing sections of water. Eggs are laid on stones in the water and the larvae, usually white or yellowish in colour, have slim bodies and grow up to 22mm long. This is a net-making species that spins a tubular silk net up to 40mm long, closed at one end and attached to rocks in the water. Prior to pupating, the larva will leave the net and make a covering of stones in which to pupate. They hatch at the end of spring and swarm in substantial numbers.

Size:	Larvae: up to 22mm. Adult: 12–15mm
Distribution:	Widespread
Habitat:	Fast-flowing sections of rivers
Hatch:	Early afternoon onwards
Season:	May–June
Description:	Larvae: White or yellowish in colour up to 22mm long
Adult:	Body and legs brown with yellow and dark brown patterned wings, long antennae

Cinnamon Sedge (*Limnephilus Lunatus*)

The Cinnamon Sedge belongs to one of the largest families of caddis fly and is very common throughout summer and into autumn. Adult flies do not swarm and may be seen on the wing from early afternoon until dusk. Hatches are somewhat sparse. The larval case, built from small pieces of plant, shells and stones is quite large and heavy; the larva is only able to crawl about slowly.

Size:	Larvae: 20–25mm. Adult: 13–15mm
Distribution:	Widespread
Habitat:	Most types of water
Hatch:	Afternoon and evening
Season:	June – October
Description:	Larvae: Case is built from plant, shells, stones and is up to 25mm long Adult: Slim looking, wings deep rich yellow/cinnamon colour with dark patterning. The anterior wings have a crescent shape on trailing edge

Grannom (*Brachycentrus subnubilus*)

This is one of the easiest of the sedge flies to recognize and is one of the first to hatch. The young larva is common in clean, running water and uses plant debris to make a square, sectioned case that becomes more cylindrical and slightly tapered as it matures. The case is fixed to stones or vegetation and the larva uses its comb-like middle legs to filter food from the water. Hatching takes place on the surface, in shallow water and adults form huge swarms over the water. The green egg sac, carried by the female at the tip of her abdomen, has given rise to the name Greentail Fly.

Size:	Larvae: up to 12mm. Adult: 9–11mm
Distribution:	Widespread but can be localized
Habitat:	Streams and rivers
Hatch:	Daytime
Season:	April and May into June
Description:	Larvae: case made of plant debris, square in section Adult: Body smoke-grey to fawn colour, fawn wings with dark mottled markings

1. Dark Caddis

DRESSING

Hook length: 9–12mm
Thread: Black
Abdomen: Dark grey-brown deer hair dubbed
Thorax: As for abdomen but picked out to represent legs
Wing: Dark brown-black coloured raffia tied tent-shaped over back

2. Traun-Wing Caddis

DRESSING

Hook length: 15–20mm
Thread: Brown
Abdomen: Brown hare's fur dubbed and picked out
Wing: Traun sedge wing cut and folded over abdomen
Hackle: Brown cock palmered full length of abdomen and left full at head

3. Elk-Hair Caddis

DRESSING

Hook length: 15–20mm
Thread: Brown
Abdomen: Hare's fur
Wing: Tan elk hair
Hackle: Brown palmered length of abdomen

4 Klinkhamen

DRESSING

Hook length: 10–20mm
Thread: Black
Abdomen: Tan poly yarn dubbed over under-body of white poly yarn
Thorax: Peacock herl
Wing: White poly yarn 'post'
Hackle: Brown cock tied parachute around wing post

5. Grannom

DRESSING

Hook length: 12mm
Thread: Green
Abdomen: Tip of fluorescent green wool, rest natural heron herl
Wing: Blue-dun cock fibres tied over abdomen
Hackle: Ginger cock

6. Grannom

DRESSING

Hook length: 12mm
Thread: Black
Abdomen: Green fluorescent floss tip, rest natural mole
Wing: Hen pheasant wing slips
Hackle: Ginger cock

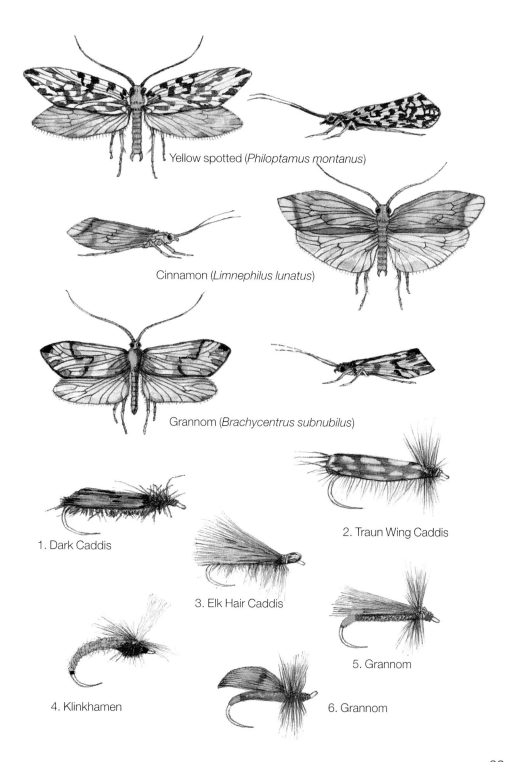

Yellow spotted (*Philoptamus montanus*)

Cinnamon (*Limnephilus lunatus*)

Grannom (*Brachycentrus subnubilus*)

1. Dark Caddis

2. Traun Wing Caddis

3. Elk Hair Caddis

4. Klinkhamen

5. Grannom

6. Grannom

Sandfly, Marbled, Small Red

Sandfly (*Rhyacophila dorsalis*)

One of the sedge flies that starts to make its appearance early in the year and is common on rapidly flowing sections of water. The larva, easily recognized by its bright green body colour, is of the free-living type. It spends its days tucked away under stones until dusk descends when it becomes quite active in its search for prey. When ready to pupate, usually late autumn, the larva builds a shelter by cementing small stones together on the underside of a large stone. Inside this shelter, a curved closed-ended cylinder, pupation takes place. When the adult fly is ready to emerge the insect bites its way out of the cocoon and swims to the surface for the final moult to take place. The adults do not tend to swarm and are mainly evening fliers.

Size:	Larva: 20–25mm. Adult: 8–16mm
Distribution:	Widely distributed
Habitat:	Common on rivers with fast to medium flows
Hatch:	Daytime
Season:	April – October
Description:	Larvae: Bright green free-living Adult: Mid-brown body with sandy to dark brown wings, speckled white

Marbled Sedge (*Hydropsyche Contubernalis*)

This is a medium-sized sedge fly which is found mostly on rivers with fast currents. Eggs are laid in round masses on the undersides of stones. The larva, which is typically arched and covered with short hairs, is extremely active. It is a net-building species spinning a net with a wide opening leading to a closed-ended tunnel. The net, which is attached to the underside of a stone, faces upstream and filters out food brought down in the flow. The net is kept clean by means of stiff hairs at the end of the abdomen. Pupation takes place in a small stone shelter built specifically for this purpose. Adult flies can often be seen in the afternoon and early evening in small groups along the river's edge.

Size:	Larvae: 18–24mm. Adult: 10–12mm
Distribution:	Fairly widespread
Habitat:	Fast-flowing water
Hatch:	Afternoon and evening
Season:	April – October
Description:	Larvae: Yellow-olive with dark segments towards head Adult: Green-bodied fly with orange legs. Wings are a basic buff colour with dark and pale brown patches

Small Red Sedge (*Tinodes Waineri*)

Amongst the smaller of our British sedges, *Tinodes* is a common fly of fast-flowing water. Like the Marbled Sedge, eggs are laid in masses on stones or other objects in the water. The larva, which has a long, thin body and short, strong legs, constructs a silk tunnel 30–40mm long which it camouflages by the addition of sand and plant detritus. This is not a carnivorous species but feeds on vegetation. The pupal shelter is constructed of sand.

Size:	Larvae: 6–8mm Adult: 8mm
Distribution:	Common and widespread
Habitat:	Fast-flowing stretches of water
Hatch:	Late afternoon and evening
Season:	May – September
Description:	Larvae: Long thin body encased in sand Adult: Grey-brown body with long, narrow, yellow-brown to red-brown wings covered with tiny hairs

1. Balloon Sedge

DRESSING

Hook length: 15–20mm
Thread: Yellow
Abdomen: Brown polypropylene dubbed
Wing: Brown deer hair
Head: Fly foam or yellow polycelon

2. Flat-Wing Sedge

DRESSING

Hook length: 15–20mm
Thread: Brown
Abdomen: Dubbed fur with brown cock hackle palmered length of body, the upper fibres cut away
Rib: Silver or gold wire
Wing: Soft feather such as partridge, coated with celluloid varnish and tied in tent-shape over body

3. V-Wing Caddis

DRESSING

Hook length: 12–16mm
Thread: Brown
Abdomen: Natural fur to suit colour
Wing: Feather tied in tent-shape over body
Hackle: Cock hackle in keeping with colour of fly

4. Little Red Sedge

DRESSING

Hook length: 10mm
Thread: Orange
Abdomen: Dark hare's fur with red cock palmered down length of body
Rib: Gold wire
Wing: Red-brown partridge tail bunched and tied over back
Hackle: Red cock tied full

5. Squirrel Tail Sedge

DRESSING

Hook length: 12–16mm
Thread: Brown
Abdomen: Cock pheasant tail fibres
Rib: Gold wire
Wing: Grey squirrel tail
Hackle: Red cock

6. Bradleys Roman Moser Caddis

DRESSING

Hook length: 12–16mm
Thread: Brown
Abdomen: Red-brown poly dubbing palmered with red cock hackle
Rib: Gold wire
Wing: Traun River Sedge wing cut to shape
Hackle: Red cock tied full then trimmed in line with lower body hackle
Antennae: Two bronze mallard fibres or similar coated with Beechams Newskin

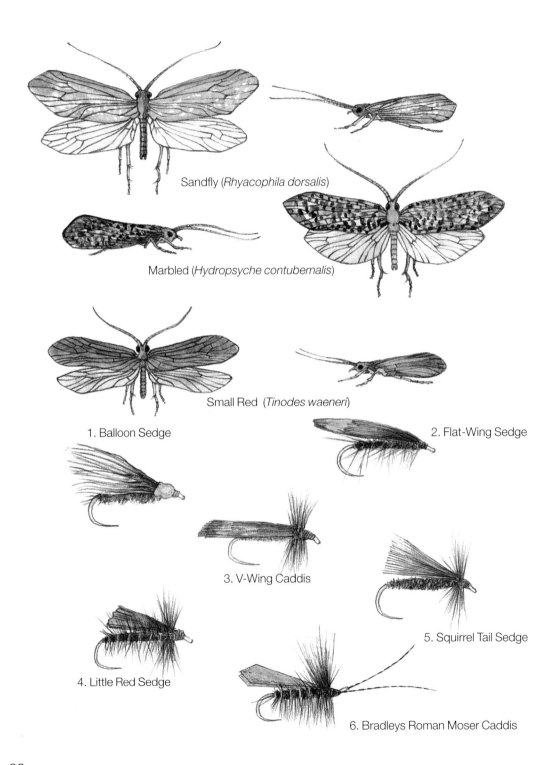

Sandfly (*Rhyacophila dorsalis*)

Marbled (*Hydropsyche contubernalis*)

Small Red (*Tinodes waeneri*)

1. Balloon Sedge

2. Flat-Wing Sedge

3. V-Wing Caddis

4. Little Red Sedge

5. Squirrel Tail Sedge

6. Bradleys Roman Moser Caddis

Grey or Silver, Brown, Brown Silverhorn

Grey or Silver Sedge (*Odontacerum Albicorne*)

This largish grey coloured fly is to be found widely distributed on fast-flowing rivers. It appears from June onwards hatching in quite sparse numbers during the daytime. One point of identification is its long, segmented antennae, each segment possessing a small tooth-like appendage.

Size: Larvae: 20mm.
 Adult: 15–18mm
Distribution: Widely distributed
Habitat: Fast-flowing rivers
Hatch: Daytime or early evening
Season: June – October
Description: Larvae: Case made from sand and gravel slightly curved and tapering
 Adult: Grey wings with darker veins and dark body

Brown Sedge (*Annabola Nervosa*)

This fly is more likely to be seen during the evenings as it spends the daytime sheltering amongst bankside vegetation. Although hatches often take place from July to October, it is during the autumn that they are at their most prolific, and on September evenings vast swarms may be seen flying over the water surface. The larva of the Brown Sedge constructs a conical case made up of small grains of sand and twigs, one of the twigs being two to three times the length of the case. The purpose of this twig is to make the case difficult to swallow and so less attractive to a feeding fish. Emergence from larva to adult usually takes place in bankside vegetation and weed beds rather than open water.

Size: Larva: 26mm.
 Adult: 11–18mm
Distribution: Widespread
Habitat: Lakes and rivers
Season: July to October
Hatch: Evenings
Description: Larvae: Case made from sand and several sticks; one of the sticks can be up to three times the length of the case
 Adult: Mid-brown wings, dark brown body

Brown Silverhorn (*Athripsodes Cinereus*)

This widely distributed fly is one of the most common of sedges and can be found on the slower reaches of many rivers and lakes. During the summer they can be observed flying in large swarms in shaded areas close to the water where feeding trout are some-times tempted to leap from the water to take one in flight. A more important source of food than the adults however are the large number of hatching pupae. Identification of the adult is assisted by the presence of very long antennae.

Size: Larvae: 12mm.
 Adult: 10mm
Distribution: Common and widespread
Habitat: Slow reaches of rivers and lakes
Hatch: Early evening
Season: June – September
Description: Larvae: Case made of fine grains of sand and with a slight curve
 Adult: Variable in colour, mostly dark brown with darker veining to wings and extremely long antennae

1. G & H Sedge

DRESSING

Hook length: 10–18mm
Thread: Green
Abdomen: Dark-green seal's fur sub under deer hair spun along body and trimmed tapering to give sedge shape
Hackle: Two rusty-dun cock hackles trimmed at the top, the stems left forward to form antennae

2. Grey Sedge

DRESSING

Hook length: 10–18mm
Thread: Grey
Abdomen: Grey seal's fur sub
Rib: Silver wire
Wing: Grey squirrel tail fibres
Hackle: Grizzle cock

3. Delta-Wing Sedge

DRESSING

Hook length: 10–18mm
Thread: Grey
Abdomen: Light-olive mink fur
Wing: Two grey hen hackle tips tied in to represent the spent female
Hackle: Brown cock with the lower fibres cut away

4. Henryville Special

DRESSING

Hook length: 10–18mm
Thread: Grey
Abdomen: Olive silk with palmered grizzle full length of body
Wing: Two grey duck quill sections either side of body over wood duck fibres
Hackle: Brown cock tied full

5. Black Sedge

DRESSING

Hook length: 10–18mm
Thread: Black
Abdomen: Black wool or chenille
Wing: Deer hair or black moose hair tied over back and clipped square
Hackle: Black cock

Sedges (Adult)

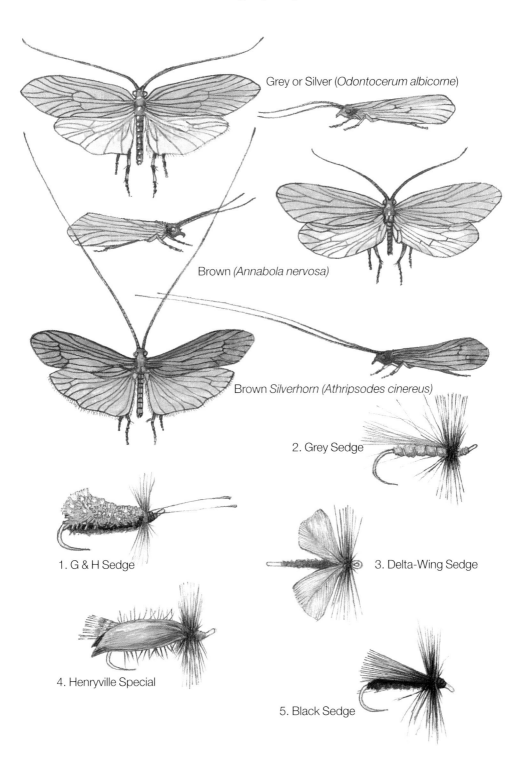

Grey or Silver (*Odontocerum albicorne*)

Brown (*Annabola nervosa*)

Brown *Silverhorn (Athripsodes cinereus)*

1. G & H Sedge

2. Grey Sedge

3. Delta-Wing Sedge

4. Henryville Special

5. Black Sedge

Caperer, Grey Flag, Welshman's Button

Caperer (*Halesus Radiatus, H. Digitatus*)

This is one of our largest sedge flies and is also one of the best known, especially on the chalkstreams of the south. Its name is derived from the female's habit of dancing or capering over the water as she lays her eggs. The larval case is a tube made from cut leaves and vegetable matter bound together by several long twigs attached longitudinally. Emergence of the adult attracts much eager attention from trout because, although hatches are not large, they do take place over a long period of time and in open water.

Size:	Larvae: Up to 30mm. Adult: 20–23mm
Distribution:	Common and widespread
Habitat:	All waters, especially chalkstreams
Hatch:	Early evening on open water
Season:	July – October
Description:	Larvae: Tube made from cut leaves and vegetable matter with several long twigs Adult: Body and legs are of orange to dark olive coloration. The broad wings are yellow and brown mottled with darker markings

Grey Flag (*Hydropsyche Instabilis*)

The Grey Flag is a very common sedge fly along fast-flowing stretches of water. Unlike many sedges, they are daytime fliers and can often be seen during the day in small groups amongst waterside vegetation. They are non-case-making species, building instead a web of silk which they use to filter micro-organisms and vegetable matter brought down to them by the current. They build a shelter on the underside of a stone in which to pupate.

Size:	Larvae: Up to 12mm. Adult: 11–12mm
Distribution:	Widely distributed
Habitat:	Fast-flowing currents
Hatch:	Daytime. Sparse
Season:	June – September
Description:	Larvae: Free-swimming, fawny-grey, net-building Adult: Fawnish-grey body with grey wings marked with lighter coloured blotches

Welshman's Button (*Sericostoma Personatum*)

This fly, of fast-running rivers and streams, was given its name by one of the greats amongst fly fishermen, F.M. Halford. It is a very common sedge and can be found in most parts of the British Isles. The larva builds a slightly curved, steeply tapering case with a characteristic smooth finish. It is constructed from tiny sand and gravel particles, the weight of which helps hold it steady in the fast-flowing water. Hatches are usually on open water and in sufficient enough numbers to cause considerable excitement amongst trout.

Size:	Larvae: 12–15mm. Adult: 12–15mm
Distribution:	Widespread and common
Habitat:	Fast-flowing water
Hatch:	Daytime and early evening
Season:	June – August
Description:	Larvae: Tube made from tiny sand and gravel particles, smooth finish and steeply tapering Adult: Dark body greenish-grey, golden-brown legs. The wings are a dark chestnut brown and covered with fine hairs. They have dark veins.

Large Cinnamon Sedge, Black Sedge, Medium Sedge, Black Silverhorns, Small Yellow Sedge, Grouse Wing (not illustrated)

Large Cinnamon Sedge (*Potamophylax Latipennis*)

A large sedge fly, fairly common, found on the wing at dusk from June to September on both stillwaters and rivers, 18–19mm. From a fishing point of view it is very similar to the Caperer and the same patterns will work.

Black Sedge (*Anthripsodes Nigronervosus*)

A medium-sized sedge fly found on both stillwater and river. Appears from June to September and is a daytime sedge. The adult is 11–13mm with slim black wings and long slender antennae. From a fishing point of view similar patterns to the Brown Sedge can be used with the alteration of colour.

Medium Sedge (*Goera Pilosa*)

Another day-flying species found between May and June, 10–12mm long, broad wings, very hairy darkish yellow to greyish yellow. Widely distributed and common, found on stillwater and river. Similar patterns to the Brown Sedge or medium-sized sedges, can be used with a suitable colour variation.

Black Silverhorns (*Mystacides Azurea, Nigra*)

A common small-sized sedge, 8–9mm long. They appear in the daytime from June to August and are mostly found on stillwaters and slow-moving rivers. They are all black with very long antennae. Black Silverhorns are very similar to Brown except for colour.

Small Yellow Sedge (*Psychomyia Pusilla*)

This is a small sedge, 5–6mm in length, yellow-brown in colour, they are found on rivers and streams swarming in large numbers mostly in the late evenings. Same patterns used for small sedges, particularly Small Red Sedge with alterations to colour.

Grouse Wing (*Mystacides Longicornis*)

Mostly a sedge of lakes and ponds, the wings are greyish with darker grey-brown markings giving a similar appearance to a grouse feather. This sedge hatches in the evenings and can be found from June to September. They have fairly long antennae and the adult is 8–10mm long. Patterns similar to the Silverhorns can be used but note the wing coloration.

1. Terry's Terror

DRESSING

Hook length: 15–20mm
Thread: Brown
Tail: Orange and yellow goat's hair, not mixed
Abdomen: Peacock herl
Rib: Flat copper tinsel
Hackle: Red cock tied full

2. Caperer

DRESSING

Hook length: 18mm
Thread: Crimson
Abdomen: Turkey tail herls separated by a band of yellow-dyed swan fibres
Wing: Dark brown feather fibres
Hackle Red cock with a black cock in front

3. Elk Hair Caddis

DRESSING

Hook length: 15–20mm
Thread: To match fly colour
Abdomen: The chosen colour from natural fur with a palmered ginger cock
Wing: Grey elk hair tied over back
Head: Elk hair roots

4. Microcaddis

DRESSING

Hook length: 7–10mm
Thread: Sparton micro or any very fine thread
Abdomen: Fine dubbing or thread
Wing: Partridge or cock hackle fibres
Hackle: Cock hackle to match colour

5. Saville's Super Sedge

DRESSING

Hook length: 20mm
Thread: Brown
Abdomen: Ostrich herl dyed cinnamon and palmered with a ginger cock
Rib: Arc yellow D.R.F. nylon floss
Wing: Hen-pheasant wing slips
Hackle: Ginger cock tied full with stalks left to form antennae

6. Spent Partridge Caddis

DRESSING

Hook length: 10–15mm
Thread: Brown
Abdomen Olive fur
Thorax: Peacock herl
Wing: Brown partridge feather fibres tied flat across back
Hackle: Brown cock palmered over thorax then trimmed top and bottom to fish in film

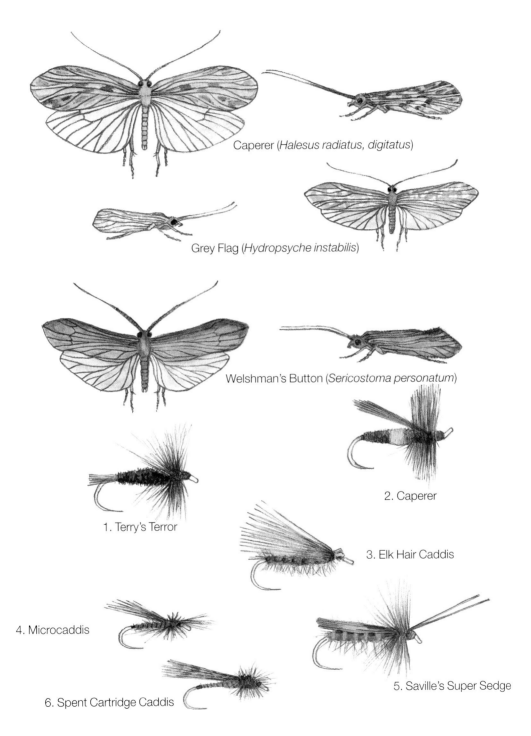

Caperer (*Halesus radiatus, digitatus*)

Grey Flag (*Hydropsyche instabilis*)

Welshman's Button (*Sericostoma personatum*)

1. Terry's Terror

2. Caperer

3. Elk Hair Caddis

4. Microcaddis

5. Saville's Super Sedge

6. Spent Cartridge Caddis

7 Stoneflies

Perla Bipunctata, Dinocras Cephalotes

Stoneflies are common waterside insects with secretive habits and a tendency to live in out-of-the-way places. Most prefer fairly fast waters where they spend their lives hiding amongst stones and waterside plants.

Stoneflies vary a great deal in size from less than ¾in up to almost 2in. All have two tails and four wings, the hind pair being broader than the front pair. The wings are hard and shiny and held flat over the body when at rest. Adult stoneflies are somewhat erratic and clumsy in flight and mating takes place on the ground or amongst vegetation. The female then returns to the water and either flies or runs over the surface depositing her eggs as she goes. The eggs then fall to the bottom where they become attached to rocks or stones. Upon hatching, the nymphs, which in some areas are known as creepers, lead a very robust and active life. They have very strong legs which enable them to cling to stones in the strong currents in which they live. As in adulthood the nymph has only two tails, this helps distinguish it from the Mayfly Nymphs which have three. Stoneflies have only three stages in their life cycle and when the nymph is ready for its transformation to adulthood it will crawl ashore for the final moult to take place.

Large Stonefly (*P. Bipunctata, D. Cephalotes*)

These two are the largest of the British Stoneflies, *Perla* being slightly larger and probably more common. Despite their large size, neither are good fliers. They both occur in roughly the same areas and appear at the same time of year.

P. Bipunctata is found in rivers with rough beds, that is, large stones but little moss or silt, whereas *Dinocras* prefers rivers with firm beds with stones partly buried and moss-covered. Both species rarely move away from the bankside where they are to be found sheltering amongst stones or vegetation.

The nymphs do show a difference in that *Perla* species are patterned black and yellow, whereas *Dinocras* is a more dusky colour. Both nymphs are carnivorous.

Size:	Larvae: 16–33mm. Adult: 16–24mm
Distribution:	Widely distributed except in Central and Southern England and East Anglia
Habitat:	*P. Bipunctata*: Swift-flowing rivers with stony bottoms *D. Cephalotes*: Swift-flowing rivers with firm bottoms
Season:	May and June
Description:	Both species are of a mottled brown appearance

1. Brown Stonefly

DRESSING

Hook length: 15–24mm
Thread: Brown
Tail: Brown goose biots
Abdomen: Brown hare's fur over lead under-body
Rib: Black Swannundaze
Thorax: Brown hare's fur
Wingcases: Turkey
Legs: Pheasant tail fibres

2. Stonefly Nymph

DRESSING

Hook length: 15–24mm
Thread: Dark brown
Tail: Stiff light-brown feather-fibres
Abdomen: Hackle stalk dyed brown over copper wire
Thorax: Copper wire covered with bronze peacock herl
Wingcases: Dark brown feather-fibres
Legs: Brown partridge

3. Brown Stonefly Nymph

DRESSING

Hook length: 15–24mm
Thread: Brown
Abdomen: Lead-foil strips on top of hook (the hook will fish upside-down) covered with brown seal's fur
Rib: Strand of amber floss
Legs: Palmered brown hen trimmed to leave only side fibres

4. Adult Stonefly

DRESSING

Hook length: 15–20mm
Thread: Brown or grey
Abdomen: Polypropylene dubbing
Rib: Grizzle cock palmered
Wing: Two grey feather slips to shape
Hackle: Natural red cock

5. Moser-Winged Stonefly

DRESSING

Hook length: 15–20mm
Thread: Brown
Abdomen: Brown polypropylene yarn
Wing: Traun River stonefly wing
Hackle: Furnace cock

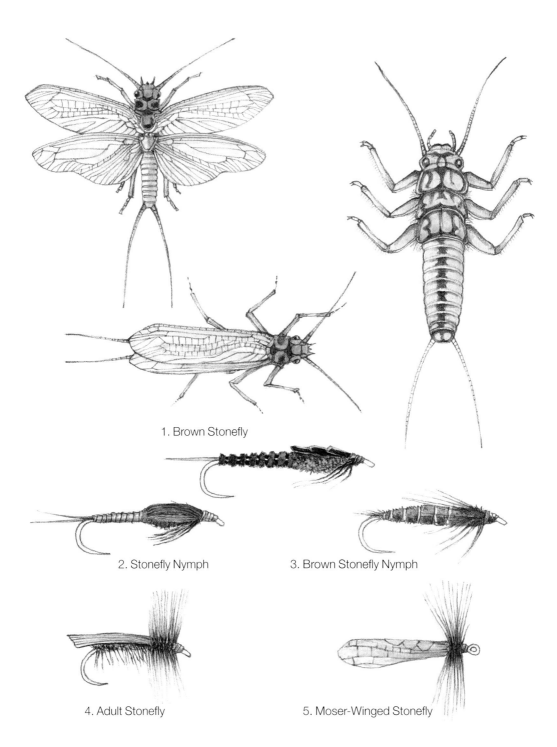

1. Brown Stonefly

2. Stonefly Nymph

3. Brown Stonefly Nymph

4. Adult Stonefly

5. Moser-Winged Stonefly

Small Brown, Small Yellow Sally, Needle Fly

Small Brown (*Nemoura Cinerea, N. Picteti*)

This small widespread stonefly has a preference for slow-flowing rivers and streams. Most of the fly's life is spent as a nymph crawling amongst moss and stones on the riverbed where it feeds on algae and other organic debris. After numerous moults the nymph leaves the water for the bankside. Here its skin splits down the back and the adult fly emerges. At first it is somewhat pale and soft and spends a period in which the wings dry out and harden off. Like all stonefly adults they eat very little and live off fats that are stored as a nymph. Eggs are laid at the surface and then sink to the bottom.

Size:	Larvae: 5–9mm. Adult: Up to 10mm
Distribution:	Widespread and common
Habitat:	Slow-flowing rivers
Season:	February – September
Description:	Larvae: Dark brown, two tails Adult: Dark brown, hard transparent wings

Small Yellow Sally (*Chloroperla Torrentium*)

This little stonefly is common in most areas of Britain and adults may be seen in flight throughout the day. The nymphs, which are found mostly on stones or amongst weeds, feed on detritus. They are slim-bodied and yellowish to reddish-brown in colour. They usually crawl out of the water when the adult is ready to emerge.

Size:	Larvae: 7–9mm Adult: 6–8mm
Distribution:	Common and widespread except in East Anglia and the Home Counties
Habitat:	Any water with sandy or stony bottom
Season:	April – August
Description:	Larvae: Slim, yellowish to reddish-brown in colour Adult: Yellow-brown body, hard yellowish wings

Needle Fly (*Leuctra Fusca, L. Hippopus*)

These two species, almost identical to look at, are the smallest of British Stoneflies. Both are exceedingly common in all areas. When at rest the wings are wrapped around the body to give a very slim appearance – hence the name Needlefly. The small, slender nymph, which is yellowish in colour, is commonly found hiding under stones or buried in sand in swift-flowing rivers.

Size:	Larvae: 6–9mm. Adult: 5–9mm
Distribution:	Widespread and common
Habitat:	Fast-flowing rivers with stony beds
Season:	*L. Fusca* August – October *L. Hippopus* February – April
Description:	Larvae: Small nymph, yellowish in colour Adult: Slim fly, dark brown in appearance

1. Brown Stonefly Nymph

DRESSING

Hook length: 10–15mm
Thread: Brown
Tail: Butts of two cock pheasant tail fibres
Abdomen: Lead foil on top of hook (to fish point up) dubbed shades of brown seal's fur sub palmered brown hen down abdomen and trimmed top and bottom
Rib: Clear nylon mono
Thorax: As for abdomen but built up with the top clear varnished (wingcases)

2. Early Brown Stonefly Nymph

DRESSING

Hook length: 10–15mm
Thread: Tan
Tail: Tan goose biots
Abdomen: Fur dubbing medium brown
Thorax: As abdomen
Wingcase: Folded dark mottled turkey to form three cases
Legs: Brown hen hackle

3. Early Brown

DRESSING

Hook length: 12mm
Thread: Red spinner
Abdomen: Brown seal's fur sub
Hackle: Slate-coloured coot palmered halfway down the body

4. Yellow Sally

DRESSING

Hook length: 8–12mm
Thread: Primrose
Tail: Light ginger cock fibres
Abdomen: Yellow and brown seal's fur sub 5:1
Rib: Primrose thread
Wings: Roman Moser Stonefly wing
Hackle: Light ginger cock

Stoneflies (Adult, Nymph)

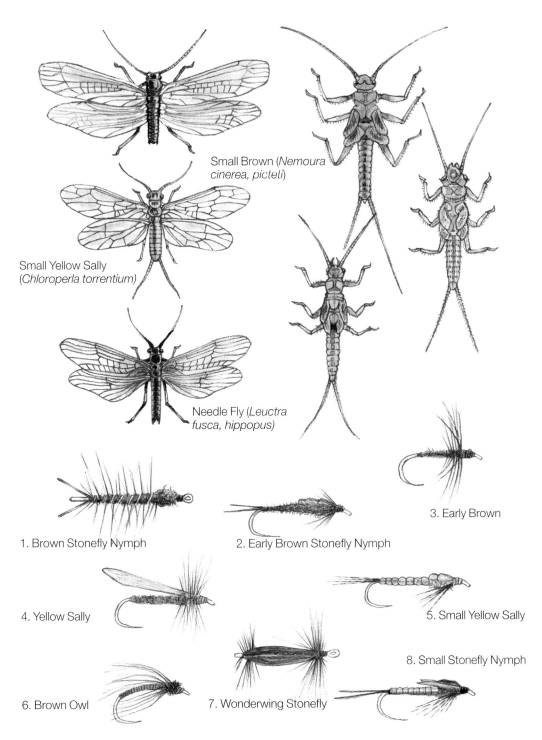

Small Brown (*Nemoura cinerea, picteli*)

Small Yellow Sally (*Chloroperla torrentium*)

Needle Fly (*Leuctra fusca, hippopus*)

3. Early Brown

1. Brown Stonefly Nymph

2. Early Brown Stonefly Nymph

4. Yellow Sally

5. Small Yellow Sally

8. Small Stonefly Nymph

6. Brown Owl

7. Wonderwing Stonefly

5. Small Yellow Sally

DRESSING

Hook length: 10–12mm
Thread: Yellow
Tail: Brown partridge hackle fibre
Abdomen: Yellow p.v.c. strip
Thorax: Yellow fur dubbing
Wingcase: Yellow p.v.c.
Legs: Brown partridge

6. Brown Owl

DRESSING

Hook length: 10–12mm
Thread: Orange
Abdomen: Orange thread
Hackle: Reddish feather
Head: Peacock herl

7. Wonderwing Stonefly

DRESSING

Hook length: 10–15mm
Thread: Hot orange
Abdomen: Dubbed Fly-Rite rust or similar
Wing: Dark red game, the fibres are pulled back flat over the abdomen, tied in, then coated with clear varnish
Hackles: Red game cock rear hackle trimmed on top, front hackle tied full

8. Small Stonefly Nymph

DRESSING

Hook length: 10–12mm
Thread: Black or brown
Tail: Two cock-pheasant tail fibres
Abdomen: Fine Swannundaze, Body Glass or brown latex
Thorax Brown dubbing
Wingcase: Goose biots, one tied over thorax, the other two tied pointing back over the abdomen
Legs: Brown partridge

February Red, Yellow Sally, Large Stonefly

February Red (*Taeniopteryx Nebulosa*)

This small fly is unusual in that it is absent from typical stonefly areas and prefers to inhabit slow-flowing stretches of water with muddy, weedy beds. In the areas it does inhabit it can be localized and present only in moderate numbers. It is an early species yet despite its name is present in greater numbers during March and April

Size:	Larvae: 10–12mm. Adult: 7–11mm
Distribution:	Localized in North Wales, Scotland and the West Country
Habitat:	Slow-flowing rivers with abundant vegetation
Season:	February – April
Description:	Larvae: Medium-small nymph, red-brown in colour Adult: Brownish body, last three segments reddish-brown. Wings brown with darker bands

Yellow Sally (*Isoperla Grammatica*)

One of a few flies that may be seen flying in bright summer sunshine. With its very conspicuous coloration it is also one of the easiest to recognize. It may be found on all kinds of lowland waters but is present in largest numbers on rivers with stony or gravelly beds. Young nymphs may be found clinging to vegetation but as they mature they prefer to creep about amongst stones on the riverbed. In some areas they may be present in equal numbers in spring and summer but in other areas they are sparse until late June.

Size:	Larvae: 11–16mm. Adult: 9–13mm
Distribution:	Fairly widespread except for East Anglia and parts of the Midlands
Habitat:	Rivers with stony or gravelly beds
Season:	April – August
Description:	Larvae: Yellow tinged brown Adult: Yellow body with yellow-brown legs and yellow green wings

Large Stonefly (*Perlodes Microcephala*)

This is another of our larger stoneflies and is common on many rivers. Although present only in small numbers and usually on faster, stonier stretches it is also the only large stonefly to occur on chalkstreams. Nymphs take about two years to reach maturity and spend their lives crawling about amongst stones on the riverbed. When the adult emergence is about to take place the nymph crawls from the water onto an exposed stone in the shallows.

In the adult male the wings are atrophied or so much reduced in size as to make flying an impossibility so it is often to be found resting in a sheltered spot near the riverbank. Although the female is capable of flight it is not very adept and so rarely takes to the air.

Size:	Larvae: up to 28mm. Adult: 13–23mm
Distribution:	Common on lowland rivers
Habitat:	Fast-flowing stretches with stony beds
Season:	April – May
Description:	Larvae: Strongly coloured with brown and yellow Adult: Mainly brown body with cream-yellow underbody and yellow-brown legs. Wings are yellow-brown with darker markings

(Larvae and Adults)

1. Dark Creeper

DRESSING

Hook length: 12–22mm
Thread: Brown
Abdomen: Brown seal's fur sub
Rib: Yellow silk
Thorax: Dark hare's ear fur
Wingcases: Dark turkey fibres
Legs: Ends of wingcases turned under body

2. Hare's Ear Stonefly Nymph

DRESSING

Hook length: 12–22mm
Thread: Brown
Tail: Dark brown grouse hackle fibres
Abdomen: Brown hare's ear
Rib: Fine gold tinsel
Thorax: Yellow fur
Wingcases: Brown partridge hackle
Legs: Brown partridge

3. February Red

DRESSING

Hook length: 10–15mm
Thread: Dark orange
Abdomen: Red-brown seal's fur sub
Wing: Grizzle cock hackle tips tied across the back
Hackle: Natural red or grizzle cock

4. February Red

DRESSING

Hook length: 10–15mm
Thread: Dark-orange
Abdomen: Mixed claret and brown seal's fur sub
Rib: Dark brown thread
Hackle: Woodcock palmered over front third

5. Yellow Sally

DRESSING

Hook length: 10-18mm
Thread: Primrose
Abdomen: Pale yellow wool or fur
Hackle: Golden Plover or pale yellow hen

6. Yellow Sally

DRESSING

Hook length: 10-15mm
Thread: Primrose
Tail: Light-ginger cock fibres
Abdomen: Yellow and brown seal's fur sub 5:1
Rib: Primrose thread
Wings: Roman Moser stonefly wings across the back
Hackle: Light-ginger cock

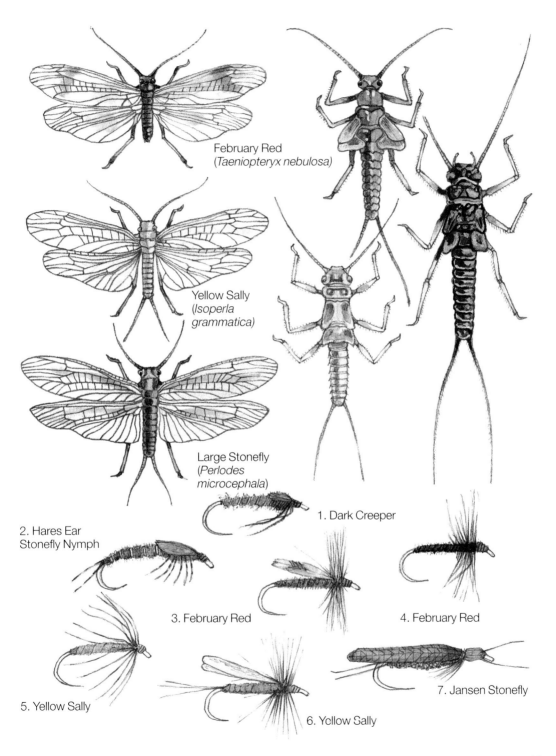

February Red
(*Taeniopteryx nebulosa*)

Yellow Sally
(*Isoperla grammatica*)

Large Stonefly
(*Perlodes microcephala*)

1. Dark Creeper

2. Hares Ear Stonefly Nymph

3. February Red

4. February Red

5. Yellow Sally

6. Yellow Sally

7. Jansen Stonefly

49

7. Jansen Stonefly

Hook length: 15–22mm
Thread: Dark brown
Tail: Hair from a pig's bristle paintbrush or similar
Abdomen: Deer hair tied in muddler style and trimmed
Wings: Synthetic curtain material coloured brown and black with waterproof markers
Legs: Dark blue dun cock fibres
Head: Clear-varnished deer hair
Antennae: As tail

Medium, Early Brown, Willow Fly (not illustrated)

Medium Stonefly (*Diura Bicaudata*)

This is a medium-sized stonefly found in localized areas mainly in the Lake District, west Wales, parts of Ireland and Scotland. It is found mostly on small stony streams and the stony edges of lakes. The adult fly is a mottled brown colour, 10–14mm in length, and appears from April until June.

Early Brown (*Protonemura Meyeri*)

This is a small stonefly being 5–9mm in length and is mostly found in the north of England. This is a fly of the early season and appears from February until May. The wings are grey-brown and the body red-brown, the head has a pale band across the top. The nymphs prefer moss-covered stones in fast water.

Willow Fly (*Leuctra Geniculata*)

A rather slim stonefly abundant and widespread over most of the country except East Anglia. They appear from August to November. The adults have brownish wings and two long antennae and are 7–10mm in length. The nymphs are found on gravel or stony river beds and it is one of the few stoneflies to be found on the chalkstreams.

8 Freshwater Shrimp/ Water Louse

Freshwater Shrimp (*Gammarus Pulex*)

Being one of our commonest crustaceans freshwater shrimp can be found in or on vegetation in most of our rivers and lakes. Its presence is a good indication of water cleanliness as it can only live where there is a high incidence of oxygen. There is no larval stage and the eggs or young shrimp are carried in a pouch on the female's body. At this time the female is carried about by the male and they are both pale reddish brown in colour. This is the breeding colour, the normal colour being greyish-brown. There is no particular breeding season and so adults can be found in large numbers throughout the year. They are very important in the trout's year-round diet.

Size: 10–20mm
Distribution: Common and widely distributed
Habitat: Clean lakes and rivers
Season: Present all year
Description: Pale reddish to greyish brown body curved in outline, mostly swims on its side

Water Louse (*Asellus Aquaticus, Meridianus*)

These non-swimming crustaceans are found in most types of water creeping about amongst decaying matter on which they feed. They are similar in appearance to wood lice but longer legged and not as solid. The eggs and young are carried about in a brood sac until sufficiently developed to be independent. As there is no set breeding time females carrying young are present at all times of the year.

Size: 12–15mm
Distribution: Common and widespread
Habitat: Muddy or weedy water
Season: Present all year
Description: Greyish-brown in colour and similar in appearance to wood lice

1. Sawyer's Killer Bug

DRESSING

Hook length: 10–20mm
Thread: None
Abdomen: Underbody of fine lead or copper wire covered with beige darning wool, grub shaped. The wire is used to weight and tie in the wool

2. Hoglouse

DRESSING

Hook length: 12–20mm
Thread: Olive
Tail: Brown Mallard/Wood duck
Abdomen: Hare's mask fur
Rib: Fine gold wire
Thorax: Oak turkey over with ends tied forward to represent feelers

3. Shrimp

DRESSING

Hook length: 10–20mm
Thread: Olive
Abdomen: Underbody of lead strips built into a hump on top of hook covered in olive wool. The back is then clear varnished
Hackle: Ginger palmered the full length with top and side fibres cut away

4. Edward's Shrimp

DRESSING

Hook length: 10–20mm
Thread: Grey
Abdomen: Lead wire bound onto the top of the hook in a hump, dubbed with a mixture of pale olive fur mixed with grey partridge hackle fibres. The back is then covered with clear polythene
Rib: Nylon mono about 4lb B.S.

5. Red Spot Shrimp

DRESSING

Hook length: 10–20mm
Thread: Olive
Abdomen: Fine lead wire dubbed olive seal's fur, olive mohair with a tuft of fluorescent red wool placed central to the fly. The back is then covered with double clear polythene
Rib: Gold wire

6. Mating Shrimp

DRESSING

Hook length: 10–20mm
Thread: Olive
Abdomen: Fine lead strips built into a hump on top of hook, dubbed with seal's fur sub 6:3:1 mix of olive, dark brown, fluorescent pink. The back is clear polythene
Rib: Oval silver wire or gold

Freshwater Shrimp (*Gammarus pulex*)
Water Louse (*Asellus aquaticus, meridianus*)

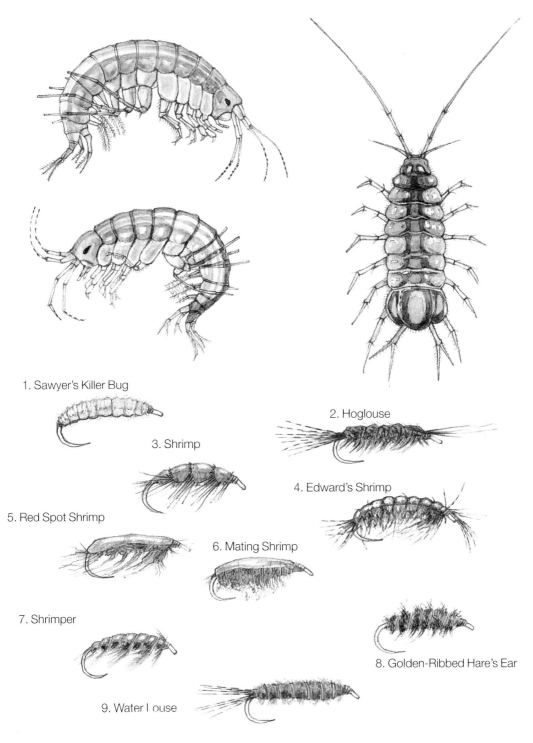

1. Sawyer's Killer Bug

2. Hoglouse

3. Shrimp

4. Edward's Shrimp

5. Red Spot Shrimp

6. Mating Shrimp

7. Shrimper

8. Golden-Ribbed Hare's Ear

9. Water Louse

7. Shrimper

DRESSING

Hook length: 10–20mm
Thread: Olive
Abdomen: Seal's fur sub, mix of olive and claret over body of fine lead wire. The back is covered with clear polythene
Rib: Fine gold wire
Hackle: Olive palmered full length

8. Gold-Ribbed Hare's Ear

DRESSING

Hook length: 10–20mm
Thread: Brown
Abdomen: Fine lead wire dubbed with short-fibred hare's ear
Rib: Fine gold wire

9. Water Louse

DRESSING

Hook length: 10–20mm
Thread: Olive
Abdomen: Fine lead wire dubbed with olive wool or seal's fur sub
Rib: Fine gold wire
Legs: Two bunches of grey partridge, tied rear facing

9 Dragonflies and Damselflies

Larvae and Adults

Dragonflies and Damselflies both belong to the order *Odonata* and have similar life cycles and occupy similar habitats. In appearance damselflies are the slimmer and more delicate looking of the two and are also the weaker fliers. It is the dragonfly with its ability to move each wing independently allowing backwards and sideways movement that provides aerial displays of extreme agility.

The wings provide us with one means of distinguishing between the insects. The damselfly has both pairs of wings similar in size and shape which, when at rest, are held along the length of the body. In the dragonfly the hind wings are larger than the forewings and when at rest the wings are held widespread.

Both dragonfly and damselfly pass through egg, nymph and adult stages but whereas the damselfly life cycle is usually completed in one year, dragonflies take anything from one to five years to complete theirs. Although adult flies of both species are occasionally taken by trout, it is the nymphal stages that are of most importance. The carnivorous nymphs spend their time feeding and growing in shallow waters with dense weed beds. When reaching maturity they move to the margins of the water in order to climb up bankside vegetation for emergence to adult to take place. At this time nymphs are very vulnerable to feeding trout.

1. Damsel Nymph

DRESSING

Hook length: 25–30mm
Thread: Green
Tail: Three olive cock hackle points
Abdomen: Seal's fur sub, ten parts olive, one dark olive, one golden olive and one white
Rib: Gold wire
Thorax: As for abdomen but no rib
Thorax Cover: Olive dyed duck fibres or similar
Legs: Olive dyed partridge feather fibres in four bunches, two each side of thorax
Eyes: Brown mono nylon melted at ends, tied in at front of thorax

2. Olive Damsel

DRESSING

Hook length: 25–30mm
Thread: Green
Tail: Three olive cock hackle points
Abdomen: Olive swan or goose herl
Rib: Fine oval gold tinsel
Thorax: Olive fur dubbing
Thorax Cover: Olive feather fibre
Legs: Olive partridge hackle
Eyes: Olive beads with black pupils

3. Green Dragon

DRESSING

Hook length: 25–30mm
Thread: Dark olive
Tail: Two goose biot tips
Abdomen: Olive dubbed S.L.F. thread
Rib: Clear mono
Thorax: Dark olive S.L.F.
Wingcase: Olive raffene
Legs: Knotted micro-chenille
Head: Olive S.L.F.
Eyes: Red chenille

4. Dubbing-Wick Dragonfly Nymph

DRESSING

Hook length: 25–30mm
Thread: Black
Tail: Short goose biot spikes
Abdomen: Two or three dubbing wicks of different colours (brown, black, green and so on) twisted together body, fatter at the rear.
Legs: Cock pheasant tail fibres
Eyes: Bead eyes to match body colours
Head: Dark brown dubbing wick

5. Blue Damsel Adult

DRESSING

Hook length: 25–30mm
Thread: Blue
Abdomen: Blue feather fibres tied long from bend to extend body, rest of abdomen dubbed blue seal's fur sub
Wings: Two badger cock hackles tied spent
Hackle: Cock dyed blue

6. Flyline Damsel

DRESSING

Hook length: 25–30mm
Thread: Black
Abdomen: Detached body made from a No. 7 or No. 8 floating line dyed blue
Rib: Black thread
Wings: Four black cock hackles tied in two groups spent
Hackle: Black or grizzle cock
Eyes: Ethafoam balls in stocking mesh tied in either side

7. Damsel Nymph

DRESSING

Hook length: 25–30mm
Thread: Green
Tail: Olive cock fibres
Abdomen: Olive green seal's fur sub
Rib: Oval gold tinsel
Thorax: As abdomen but fatter
Wingcases: Cock pheasant tail fibres over thorax with tips sticking out either side
Legs: Hen-pheasant tail fibres

Dragonflies and Damselflies
(Larvae and Adults) (*Odonata*)

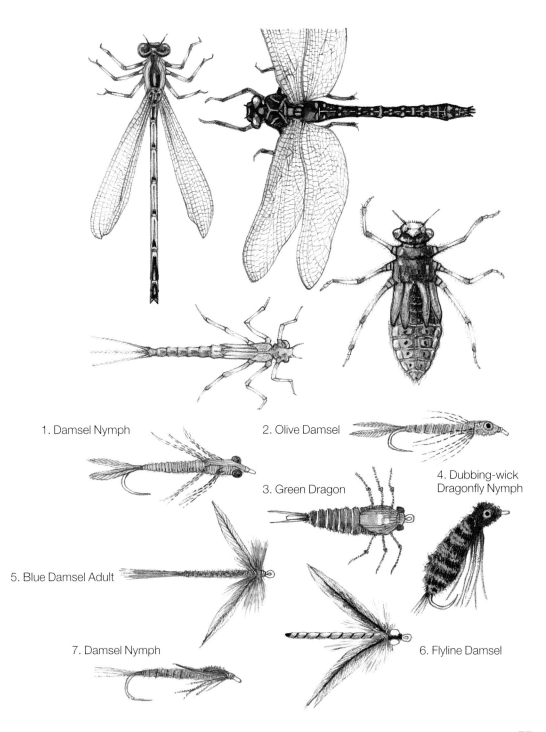

1. Damsel Nymph

2. Olive Damsel

3. Green Dragon

4. Dubbing-wick Dragonfly Nymph

5. Blue Damsel Adult

6. Flyline Damsel

7. Damsel Nymph

10 Ephemeroptera

(Nymphs) 1

The nymph is the second stage in the life cycle of the upwinged flies (*Ephemeroptera*) following the egg. The nymph stage depending on the species may last from a few months or up to two years as is the case with *E. Danica*, the Mayfly.

During this time the nymphs will live close to the river or lake bottom. Some will live by burrowing into the mud on the bottom, others will spend their lives crawling amongst the weeds and stones. Some species move about in the water very quickly and some with a very slow deliberate motion.

Throughout the life of the nymph, growth is made through a series of moults. With the last moult the wings will be fully formed beneath the nymphal skin and the mature nymph is ready to rise to the surface and hatch into the dun.

Claret Dun, Sepia Dun (*Leptophlebia*)

A slow-moving type nymph, found in both still and slow-moving water. It has a narrow body, yellowish-brown in colour, gills feathery leaf-shaped, 7–12mm long.

Dark Olive, Iron Blue, Lake Olive, Large Dark Olive, Medium Olive, Pale Watery, Pond Olive, Small Dark Olive, Large Spurwing, Small Spurwing (*Baetis (Cloeon) (Centroptilum)*)

Agile, darting-type nymph found in still, slow-moving and faster flows depending on species. Narrow body ranging in colour from yellow-green through olives to browns, gills oval-shaped, 5–10mm long.

Caenis, 'Broadwings, Angler's Curse' (*Caenis*)

Mud-dwelling type nymph, found in lakes and rivers. Body small not flattened at all, mostly yellowish-brown in colour, gills not obvious.

Blue-Winged Olive, Yellow Evening Dun (*Ephemerella*)

Moss-creeping type nymph, found in all types of rivers. The Blue-Winged Olive is also found in some larger lakes. Body very slightly flattened, yellowish-dark brown in colour, gills very small. Only four pairs are visible.

Nymphs 1

1. Claret Nymph

Hook length: 10–18mm
Thread: Brown
Tail: Black hen fibres
Abdomen: Dark brown seal's fur sub mixed with a little ginger fur
Rib: Silver wire
Thorax: Black seal's fur
Legs: Dark brown hen

2. Claret Nymph

Hook length: 10–18mm
Thread: Black
Tail: Three strands of brown mallard
Abdomen: Dark claret seal's fur sub picked out at sides
Rib: Gold wire
Thorax: Black seal's fur sub
Wingcase: Black goose quill
Legs: Brown partridge

3. Sepia Nymph

Hook length: 10–18mm
Thread: Black
Tail: Cock-pheasant tail fibres
Abdomen: Black sheep's wool picked out at the sides
Rib: Black floss silk
Thorax: Black sheep's wool
Wingcase: Cock-pheasant tail fibres
Legs: Cock-pheasant tail fibres swept back either side of thorax

4. Large Dark Olive Nymph

Hook length: 10–18mm
Thread: Yellow
Tail: Dark olive cock hackle fibres
Abdomen: Dark olive fur
Rib: Gold wire
Thorax: Brown seal's fur sub
Wingcase: Dark olive goose quill
Legs: Fibres from wingcase tied either side of thorax

5. Olive Nymph

Hook length: 10–18mm
Thread: Yellow
Tail: Olive cock hackle fibres
Abdomen: Yellow-olive seal's fur sub
Rib: Gold wire
Thorax: Brown fur
Wingcase: Light pheasant tail fibres
Legs: Tips of pheasant tail fibres left either side of thorax

6. Large Dark Olive Nymph

Hook length: 10–18mm
Thread: Dull orange
Tail: Badger hair dyed medium olive
Abdomen: Olive flexibody in overlapping turns
Wingcases: Dark turkey feather fibres with a strip of abdomen material down the centre
Legs: Small speckled partridge feather dyed medium olive
Thorax: Olive-brown hare's belly fur

7. Medium Olive Nymph

DRESSING

Hook length: 10–18mm
Thread: Primrose
Tail: Blue-dun cock hackle fibres
Abdomen: Olive dyed heron herl
Rib: Fine gold wire
Thorax: Blue squirrel's fur
Hackle: Short fibred blue-dun cock

8. Caenis Nymph

DRESSING

Hook length: 7–12mm
Thread: Brown
Tail: Three brown partridge hackle fibres
Abdomen: Goose or heron herl
Rib: Stripped peacock quill
Thorax: Hare's ear fur
Wingcases: Biot quills from a heron
primary feather
Legs: Partridge fibres

9. Iron Blue Spider

DRESSING

Hook length: 7–12mm
Thread: Crimson
Tip: Crimson thread
Abdomen: Lightly dubbed mole's fur
Hackle: Hackle from moorhen's wing or snipe

10. Iron Blue Nymph

DRESSING

Hook length: 7–12mm
Thread: Claret
Tail: White cock fibres
Tip: Claret thread
Abdomen: Mole's fur
Thorax: Mole's fur
Wing Case: Black crow
Leg: Wingcase fibres tied beneath the body

11. Caenis Nymph

DRESSING

Hook length: 7–12mm
Thread: Brown
Tail: Three blue-dun hackle fibres
Abdomen: Tan fur dubbed
Rib: Brown thread
Thorax: Tan fur picked out for legs
Wingcase: Blue-dun hackle fibres tied over
thorax

12. Blue-Winged Olive Nymph

DRESSING

Hook length: 10–15mm
Thread: Hot orange
Tail: Brown-speckled partridge hackle fibres
Abdomen: Rust Antron/hare blend
Thorax: A mixture of red and black
seal's fur sub
Hackle: Small dark blue-dun hen hackle

Nymphs (*Ephemeroptera*)

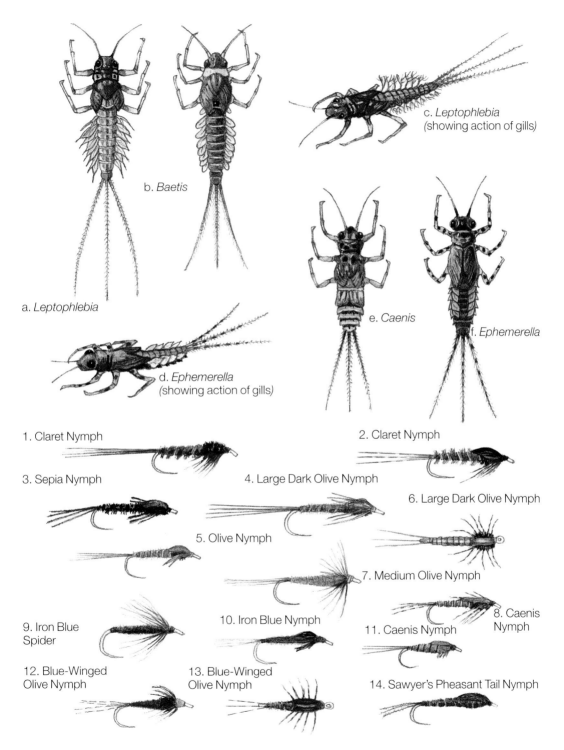

b. *Baetis*

c. *Leptophlebia*
(showing action of gills)

a. *Leptophlebia*

d. *Ephemerella*
(showing action of gills)

e. *Caenis*

f. *Ephemerella*

1. Claret Nymph

2. Claret Nymph

3. Sepia Nymph

4. Large Dark Olive Nymph

6. Large Dark Olive Nymph

5. Olive Nymph

7. Medium Olive Nymph

9. Iron Blue Spider

10. Iron Blue Nymph

11. Caenis Nymph

8. Caenis Nymph

12. Blue-Winged Olive Nymph

13. Blue-Winged Olive Nymph

14. Sawyer's Pheasant Tail Nymph

13. Blue-Winged Olive Nymph

Hook length: 10–15mm
Thread: Orange
Tail: Dark mottled partridge tail
Abdomen: Sandy hare's ear fur
Rib: Fine gold wire abdomen only
Thorax: Sandy hare's ear fur
Legs: Dark partridge hackle
Wingcase: Dark pheasant tail fibres tied in two strips over thorax leaving hare's ear showing down centre

14. Sawyer's Pheasant Tail Nymph

Hook length: 10–18mm
Thread: Pheasant tail fibres
Tail: Three cock pheasant tail fibres
Abdomen: Underbody: Copper wire with a humped thorax
Overbody: Pheasant tail fibre wound on with copper wire
Wingcase: Pheasant tail fibres doubled and redoubled

Nymphs 2

Autumn Dun, Dusky Yellow-streak, Large Brook Dun, Large Green Dun, Late March Brown, Yellow May Dun (*Ecdyonurus (Heptagenia)*)

Stone-clinger type nymph, found in rivers and lakes depending on species. Body broad and flattened. Yellowish-brown to dark-brown with obvious markings. Gills oval in shape, 8–15mm long.

March Brown, Olive Upright (*Rhithrogena*)

Stone-clinger type nymph, found in mostly stony rivers. Body broad and flattened, yellowish-green to yellowish-brown, gills oval in shape, 8–12mm long.

Potamanthidae (No common name)

Stone-clinger type nymph, found mostly in large rivers in the side pools and margins with a sand or stony bottom. Slimmish body, yellowish with brown markings, gills double-branched and feather-like, 10–12mm long.

Large Summer Dun (*Siphlonurus*)

Agile, darting type nymph, found mostly in lakes and slow-flowing sections of rivers. Slim large nymphs brown-olive in colour, gills, the first six gills are double plates slightly heart-shaped, the last gill is single. The nymph is up to 18mm long.

1. March Brown Nymph

DRESSING

Hook length: 10–18mm
Thread: Brown
Tail: Three strands of brown mallard flank fibres
Abdomen: Brown fur dubbing
Rib: Gold wire
Thorax: Brown fur
Legs: Speckled grouse hackle
Wingcase: Woodcock quill fibres

2. March Brown Spider

DRESSING

Hook length: 10–15mm
Thread: Brown or primrose
Tail: Speckled partridge tail fibres
Abdomen: Dark hare's ear fur mixed with claret seal's fur sub (4:1)
Rib: Silver wire
Hackle: Speckled partridge

3. March Brown Nymph

DRESSING

Hook length: 10–18mm
Thread: Black or brown
Tail: Three cock-pheasant tail fibres
Abdomen: Hare's fur and Antron mix
Thorax: Hare's fur and Antron mix
Legs: Partridge hackle
Back/Wing Case/Head: Mottled turkey strip treated with flexible cement
Rib: Fine gold wire

4. March Brown Nymph

DRESSING

Hook length: 10–18mm
Thread: Brown
Tail: Three widely spaced cock pheasant tail fibres
Abdomen: Cock pheasant tail fibres
Rib: Gold wire
Thorax: Hare's ear fur picked out at sides only
Wingcase: Woodcock wing feather fibres
Legs: Brown speckled partridge hackle

5. Loop-Wing Emerger

DRESSING

Hook length: 10–18mm
Thread: Orange
Tail: Widely spaced cree cock fibres
Abdomen: Mixed rabbit's fur and poly dubbing dyed olive
Wing: Upright loop of tan polypropylene yarn
Legs: Cree cock fibres tied either side of abdomen

6. Suspender Nymph

DRESSING

Hook length: 10–18mm
Thread: Brown
Tail: Greenwell cock hackle fibres
Abdomen: Goose feather fibres dyed olive
Rib: Fine gold tinsel or wire
Thorax: Dark-olive seal's fur
Wingcase: Brown feather fibres, the tips are tied under for legs
Suspender ball: Small ethafoam ball in nylon mesh. This acts as float and emerging adult

Nymphs (*Ephemeroptera*)

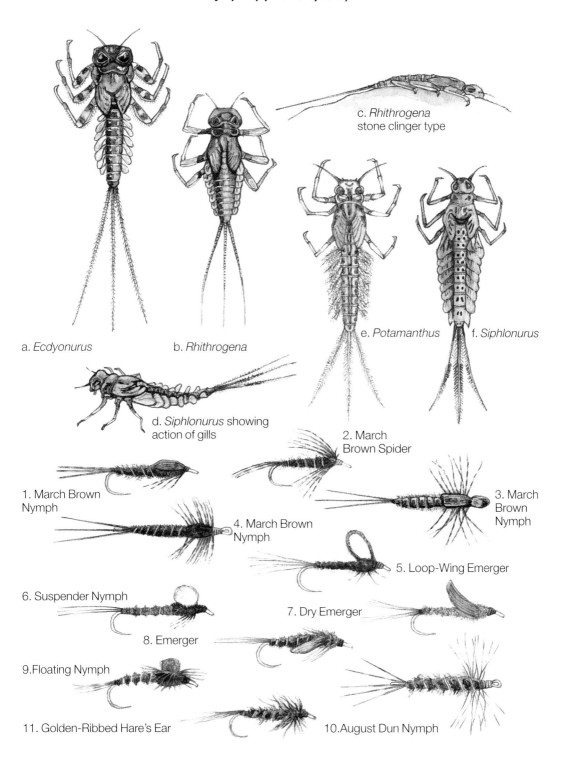

a. *Ecdyonurus*

b. *Rhithrogena*

c. *Rhithrogena* stone clinger type

d. *Siphlonurus* showing action of gills

e. *Potamanthus*

f. *Siphlonurus*

1. March Brown Nymph

2. March Brown Spider

3. March Brown Nymph

4. March Brown Nymph

5. Loop-Wing Emerger

6. Suspender Nymph

7. Dry Emerger

8. Emerger

9. Floating Nymph

10. August Dun Nymph

11. Golden-Ribbed Hare's Ear

7. Dry Emerger

DRESSING

Hook length: 10–18mm
Thread: Olive
Tail: Ginger cock hackle fibres
Abdomen: Dubbed olive-brown fur
Wing: Short tied grey-duck quills

8. Emerger

DRESSING

Hook length: 10–18mm
Thread: Crimson
Tail: Light-blue dun cock fibres
Abdomen: Mixed rabbit and mole's fur
Rib: Stripped quill
Wing: Two short rear facing grey mallard slips tied either side of thorax
Hackle: Lemon wood duck tied in front of wing slips and sloping backwards

9. Floating Nymph

DRESSING

Hook length: 10–15mm
Thread: Dark brown
Tail: Wood duck fibres
Abdomen: Dark-olive Antron and hair mix built up at thorax
Rib: White p.v.c. strip
Thorax: As abdomen with a dubbed ball of grey polypropylene on top
Hackle: Parachute Golden-olive cock wound round bottom of grey polypropylene ball

10. August Dun Nymph

DRESSING

Hook length: 10–18mm
Thread: Yellow
Tail: Yellow guinea-fowl fibres
Abdomen: Brown and yellow seal's fur sub, well picked out
Rib: Fine gold wire
Hackle: Golden plover tied in over thorax area and trimmed top and bottom

11 Gold-Ribbed Hare's Ear

DRESSING

Hook length: 10–18 mm
Thread: Brown
Tail: Guard hairs
Abdomen: Dark hare's ear fur
Rib: Fine flat gold tinsel
Thorax: As abdomen
Legs: Thorax fibres well picked out

11 Ephemeroptera

Pale Watery, Small Dark Olive, Yellow Evening Dun (Adult) 1

Pale Watery (*Baetis Fuscatus*)

This medium-sized fly is common on most chalk and limestone rivers of England and Wales and has a preference for running water. The female of the species is probably one of the hardest of the *baetids* to identify being very similar to others of the 'olive' group. The male is easily distinguished by his yellow eyes. In the past, several species were referred to as 'pale watery' but today *fuscatus, bioculatus* is usually the one meant. The nymph is a very agile swimmer found living in weed beds. It has three tails, the middle one being slightly shorter than the other two. In the evenings adult males may be seen swarming along banksides and many fall to the water surface. The female crawls down into the water to lay her eggs and many die trapped beneath the surface film.

Size:	Nymph: 11mm.
	Adult: 6–8mm
Distribution	Common on most limestone and chalk areas of England and Wales
Habitat:	Alkaline rivers with good weed growth
Hatch:	Daytime
Season:	May – October (highest incidence – May and June)
Description:	Nymph: Very pale yellowish olive with three tails
	Dun: Female:Pale grey wings. Pale olive body with last two segments yellow-olive. Dark-grey to lower part of legs. Male similar to female but yellow eyes
	Spinner: Female: Golden olive

body, the last three segments being a shade darker. Two tails, transparent wings. Male: Creamy olive body, transparent wings, yellow eyes

Small Dark Olive (*Baetis Scambus*)

Amongst the smallest of the upwinged flies, the small dark olive is only to be found in running water. The very small nymph is usually found in weed beds but may also be present in moss or stones on the river bed. It is a very agile swimmer of slim appearance with long tails fringed with hairs. Adult males may be seen swarming in large numbers under bankside vegetation but do not form an important part of a trout's diet – it is the female spinner which fulfils this role. The fertilized female crawls beneath the surface of the water to lay her eggs on submerged stones. In order to breathe she carries air trapped under her wings. When egg laying is completed many of the flies are too weak to break back through the surface film and so die trapped beneath the water where they provide very easy and welcome food for feeding trout.

Size:	Nymph: up to 9mm.
	Adult: 4–6mm
Distribution:	Widespread, except Ireland and Scotland
Habitat:	Medium to fast-flowing water
Season:	May – September, peak July – August
Hatch:	Afternoon – evening
Description:	Nymph: Slender, pale yellowy olive

Dun: Medium grey wings with a pale olive body
Spinner: Reddish-brown body with yellowish tails, transparent wings

Yellow Evening Dun (*Ephemerella Notata*)

This appears to be an upwinged fly that is on the decline and is now only found in localized areas of Britain where it seems to prefer slower stretches of running water. Nymphs are poor swimmers and spend their time crawling about in the mud and weed on the bottom where they cover themselves with debris. Duns, which have three tails, make their appearance in May and June.

Size: Nymph: 12–14mm.
Adult: 10–12mm
Distribution: Localized in Ireland, central Wales and N.W. England

Habitat: Running water with dense weed
Hatch: Late evening
Season: May and June
Description: Nymph: Yellow-brown body slightly flattened, found amongst weeds
Dun: Female: Yellow body with pale yellow legs, pale yellow wings with yellowish veining. Pale green eyes. Male: Pale yellow body, the last three segments being light amber. Pale grey wings with yellowish veining. Yellow legs, orange eyes
Spinner: Female: Yellow olive body, the last three segments brown-olive. Olive-yellow legs, wings transparent with a yellow leading edge, greenish eyes. Male similar to female but with orange eyes

1. Pale Watery Dun

DRESSING

Hook length: 8–10mm
Thread: Primrose
Tail: Honey-dun fibres
Abdomen: Tip primrose tying thread, rest swan herl tinted pale greenish-grey
Hackle: Honey-dun

2 Pale Watery Dun

DRESSING

Hook length: 8–10mm
Thread: Light yellow
Tail: Honey-dun
Abdomen: Tip yellow tying thread, rest light-grey heron herl or goose dyed pale olive
Hackle: Honey-dun

3. Goddard's Last Hope

DRESSING

Hook length: 8–10mm
Thread: Pale yellow
Tail: Dark honey-dun fibres
Abdomen: Buff-coloured condor herl sub or goose breast feather fibres
Hackle: Short-fibred dark honey-dun cock

4. Pale Watery Spinner

DRESSING

Hook length: 8–10mm
Thread: Cream
Tail: Honey hackle fibres
Abdomen: Stripped yellow hackle stalk
Thorax: Ginger Antron
Wing: Cream poly yarn tied spent

5. Yellow Evening Dun

DRESSING

Hook length: 10–14mm
Thread: Hot orange
Tail: Ginger cock fibres
Abdomen: Orange rayon floss
Rib: Gold wire
Wing: Tied forward over eye bunch of yellow cock fibres
Hackle: Ginger cock

6. Lunn's Yellow Boy

DRESSING

Hook length: 10–14mm
Thread: Pale orange
Tail: Pale-buff cock fibres
Abdomen: White hackle stalk dyed yellow or yellow seal's fur sub
Wing: Pale-buff cock hackle fibred bunched and tied spent

7. Yellow Evening Spinner

DRESSING

Hook length: 10–14mm
Thread: Orange
Tails: Yellow or cream cock fibres
Abdomen: Pale yellow-olive seal's fur sub tying thread showing as tip at rear
Wing: Honey cock fibres tied in spent position

8. Small Dark Olive Spinner

DRESSING

Hook length: 6–8mm
Thread: Brown
Tails: Two widely spaced sparse bunches of pale blue-dun fibres
Abdomen: Rusty-red seal's fur sub
Wing: Pale blue-dun cock tied spent

9. Pheasant Tail

DRESSING

Hook length: 10–12mm
Tail: Honey-dun hackle fibres
Abdomen: Cock pheasant centre tail fibres
Rib: Gold wire
Hackle: Honey-dun cock

10. Small Dark Olive Dun

DRESSING

Hook length: 6–8mm
Thread: Yellow
Tail: Blue-dun cock fibres
Abdomen: Mixed light-olive and Adam Grey Fly-Rite 15 and 26 dub
Hackle: Olive cock with blue-dun in front

11. Pheasant Tail Spinner

DRESSING

Hook length: 10mm
Tail: Honey-dun cock fibres
Abdomen: Cock pheasant centre tail fibres
Rib: Gold wire
Hackle: Honey-dun cock tied parachute

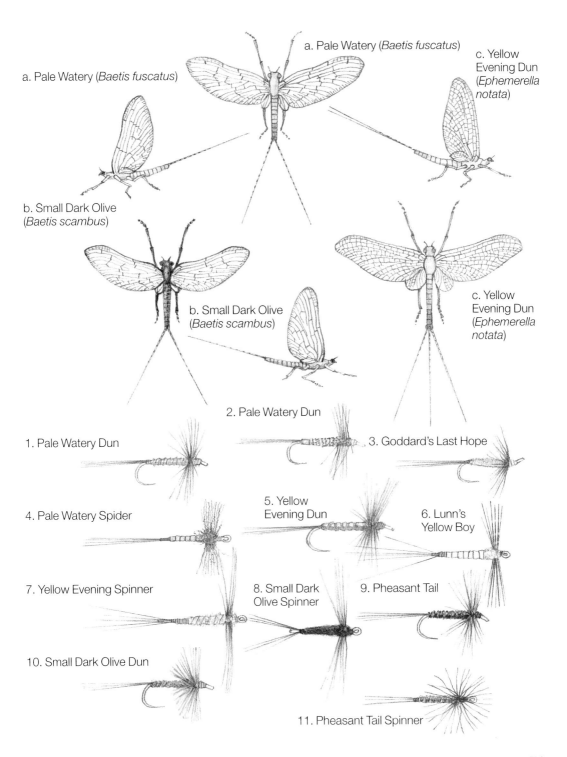

a. Pale Watery (*Baetis fuscatus*)

a. Pale Watery (*Baetis fuscatus*)

c. Yellow Evening Dun (*Ephemerella notata*)

b. Small Dark Olive (*Baetis scambus*)

b. Small Dark Olive (*Baetis scambus*)

c. Yellow Evening Dun (*Ephemerella notata*)

2. Pale Watery Dun

1. Pale Watery Dun

3. Goddard's Last Hope

4. Pale Watery Spider

5. Yellow Evening Dun

6. Lunn's Yellow Boy

7. Yellow Evening Spinner

8. Small Dark Olive Spinner

9. Pheasant Tail

10. Small Dark Olive Dun

11. Pheasant Tail Spinner

Caenis, Autumn Dun, Blue Winged Olive (Adult) 2

Angler's Curse (*Caenis Species*)

This group of very small flies are known as the Angler's Curse on account of the difficulty encountered catching fish when they are hatching. There are six species of *Caenis* all of which are very common and abundant and may be found in any type of water. Nymphs that are often less than 9mm long and partly carnivorous, inhabit the bottom mud where they crawl about in search of food.

A unique feature of these tiny flies is their ability to moult extremely rapidly. This transformation can easily be observed as they hatch in vast numbers and will alight on any convenient object, including the angler. As soon as the dun emerges at the water's surface it will fly to land and almost immediately moult again into the spinner. Within another minute or two the spinner takes to the air in order to mate. Soon after mating the female will return to the water to deposit her eggs.

Size:	Nymph: up to 9mm. Adult: Mostly less than 4mm
Distribution:	Common and widespread
Habitat:	Any type of water
Hatch:	Early morning or evening
Season:	June to September
Description:	Nymph: Mottled brown, short, stout body Dun: Creamy body,broad wings, no hindwings,three tails Spinner: Creamy body, dark brown thorax, broad wings, no hindwings, three tails can be very long

Autumn Dun (*Ecdyonorus Dispar*)

This somewhat localized fly was once known as the August Dun as this is the month in which the most prolific hatches occur. It is a rather large fly with a preference for fast-flowing stony rivers. The nymph, with its broad, flat body and large, flat limbs, is adapted for life in the strong currents. Living at the bottom clinging to stones with its strong, clawed feet, it is able to move rapidly over the surface and is a strong swimmer when necessary. Emergence of the dun may take place at the surface in open water or sometimes the nymph will crawl onto a stone in the shallows.

Male spinners can often be seen swarming at the river's edge and many end up being blown onto the surface. Fertilized females rest on stones in the shallows, pushing their abdomens beneath the surface and attaching their eggs to the sides or underneath submerged stones.

Size:	Nymph: 16–18mm. Adult: 12–14mm
Distribution:	Fairly common in the North, the West Country and Wales
Habitat:	Fast-flowing, stony rivers and lakes
Hatch:	Daytime
Season:	August, September
Description:	Nymph: Dark brown and tan mottled, three tails Dun: Female: pale olive brown body, fawn heavily veined wings, two tails. Male: yellow olive body with dark brown bands, grey heavily veined wings, greenish-brown eyes, two tails Spinner: Female: reddish-brown body, transparent wings with dark veining, greenish-brown eyes, known as 'The Great Red Spinner'. Male: reddish- brown body, transparent wings, brown veining

Blue Winged Olive (*Ephemerella Ignita*)

Probably the most common and easy to recognize of the upwinged flies, it can be found almost everywhere and in all kinds of flowing water. Adults begin to appear in mid-June and are present throughout the season, in fact they have been recorded in every month of the year.

Nymphs, which are moss creepers, inhabit the submerged weed beds and mosses on the faster flowing stretches of water. They have a slightly flattened dark body, lighter underneath and strong legs. Emergence takes place in open water usually from late afternoon to early evening and can go on until dusk so it is possible for both dun and spinner to be present on the water at the same time.

Size:	Nymph: 14mm. Adult: 10mm
Distribution:	Widespread and abundant
Habitat:	All types of flowing water
Hatch:	Evening
Season:	May – October
Description:	Nymph: dark reddish-brown Dun: Female: green-olive changing to brown-olive later, dark blue-grey wings, three tails. Male: dark brown-olive body, dark blue-grey wings, red eyes, three tails
Spinner:	Sherry red body, transparent wings, brown veining, greenish-brown eyes, 'Sherry Spinner'. Male: dark brown to red-brown body, transparent wings, light brown veining, bright red eyes

1. Caenis Dun

DRESSING

Hook length: 5–7mm
Thread: White midge thread
Tail: Cream cock fibres
Abdomen: Mole's fur
Thorax: Stripped black ostrich herl, shiny side out
Hackle: Tiny dark blue dun cock

2. Last Hope

DRESSING

Hook length: 5–7mm
Thread: Pale yellow
Tail: Dark honey-dun fibres
Abdomen: Buff-coloured condor herl sub or goose breast feather fibres
Hackle: Dark honey-dun cock

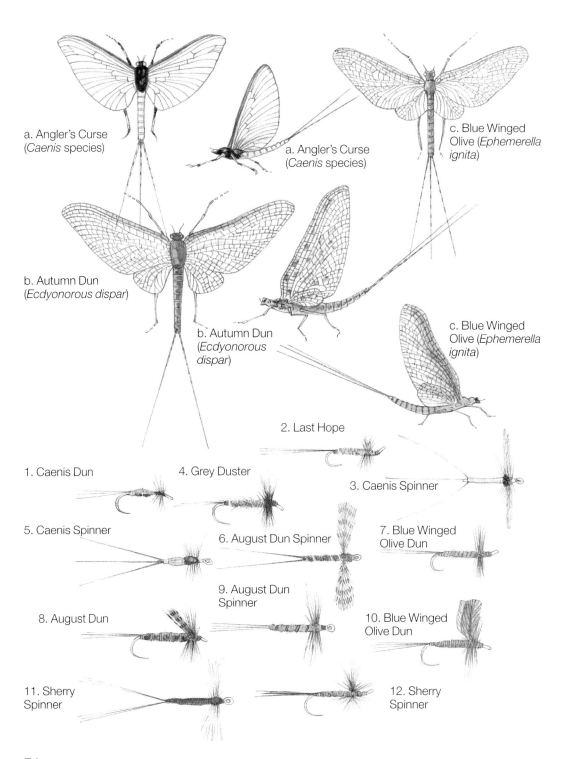

a. Angler's Curse
(*Caenis* species)

a. Angler's Curse
(*Caenis* species)

c. Blue Winged
Olive (*Ephemerella
ignita*)

b. Autumn Dun
(*Ecdyonorous dispar*)

b. Autumn Dun
(*Ecdyonorous
dispar*)

c. Blue Winged
Olive (*Ephemerella
ignita*)

2. Last Hope

1. Caenis Dun

4. Grey Duster

3. Caenis Spinner

5. Caenis Spinner

6. August Dun Spinner

7. Blue Winged
Olive Dun

9. August Dun
Spinner

8. August Dun

10. Blue Winged
Olive Dun

11. Sherry
Spinner

12. Sherry
Spinner

3. Caenis Spinner

DRESSING

Hook length: 5–7mm
Thread: White midge thread
Tail: Three wide spaced white cock fibres
Abdomen: White polythene
Thorax: Brown condor herl sub or turkey
Wing: White hen hackle cut small and tied spent
Hackle: Short–fibred white cock trimmed flat on bottom

4. Grey Duster

DRESSING

Hook length: 5–12mm
Thread: Brown
Tail: Badger cock fibres
Abdomen: Blue-grey rabbit's fur
Hackle: Badger cock

5. Caenis Spinner

DRESSING

Hook length: 5–7mm
Thread: White midge thread
Tail: Three wide spaced Microfibetts
Abdomen: Cream-dyed rabbit's fur or similar
Thorax: Brown-black rabbit's fur
Hackle: Small, very pale blue dun or white cock trimmed on top and bottom

6. August Dun Spinner

DRESSING

Hook length: 12–15mm
Thread: Claret
Tail: Brown Microfibetts
Abdomen: Reddish-brown seal's fur sub
Rib: Fine gold wire
Wing: Two light partridge breast feathers tied in spent

7. Blue Winged Olive Dun

DRESSING

Hook length: 10mm
Thread: Yellow
Tail: Blue-dun hackle fibres
Abdomen: Pinkish-beige opossum fur or similar
Hackle: Blue-dun with red game at front

8. August Dun

DRESSING

Hook length: 12– 15mm
Thread: Brown
Tail: Ginger-brown cock fibres
Abdomen: Brown floss or brown quill
Rib: Yellow floss
Wing: Mottled hen-pheasant
Hackle: Ginger-brown cock

9. August Dun Spinner

Hook length: 12–15mm
Thread: Hot orange
Tail: Honey-dun fibres
Abdomen: Orange seal's fur sub
Rib: Thread
Hackle: Red cock

10. Blue-Winged Olive Dun

Hook length: 10mm
Thread: Olive
Tail: Dark-dun cock fibres
Abdomen: Dark olive rabbit's fur
Wing: Grey duck wing quills
Hackle: Dark-dun cock

11. Sherry Spinner

Hook length: 10–12mm
Thread: Sherry Spinner
Tail: Two wide spaced bunches cock fibres or two white Microfibetts
Abdomen: Red-brown seal's fur sub
Wing: White poly yarn bunched, tied in spent

12. Sherry Spinner

Hook length: 10–12mm
Thread: Yellow
Tail: Natural buff cree fibres
Abdomen: Tip of yellow rayon floss then two moose mane hairs dyed, one dark, the other sherry (pinkish-red) and wound on segmented
Wing: Pale ginger cock fibres tied bunched and spent
Hackle: Natural red cock

Large Dark Olive, Iron Blue, Medium Olive (Adult) 3

Large Dark Olive (*Baetis Rhodani*)

Another of the upwinged flies which is common to all parts of the country and can be found on all types of river, although its preference is for faster flowing stretches. Early spring and late autumn are the times when hatches of any significance occur and it is the earliest upwinged fly to be present in sufficient numbers to be of interest to trout.

The nymph is an agile darter spending its time amongst weeds and stones of the river bed.

Emergence takes place at the surface in open water and duns often get trapped in the surface film before their wings are dry enough to get them airborne, so providing an easy meal for a hungry trout. Because of its red-brown body the female spinner is often referred to as the 'Large Red Spinner'. Adults have only tiny hindwings and two tails.

Size:	Nymph: 10–14mm. Adult: 7–10mm
Distribution:	Widespread on most types of river
Habitat:	Any flowing water
Hatch:	Daytime
Season:	March – April and September – October
Description:	Nymph: Dark olive body with pale yellow segmentation Dun: Medium-dark olive body, pale grey wings, greenish eyes. Male as female but reddish eyes Spinner: Female: Red-brown body, transparent wings. Male: Pale olive body, last three segments orange-brown, transparent wings

Iron Blue (*Baetis Niger, Muticus*)

This, the smallest of the early spring upwings, is common to all parts except S.E. England. Hatches occur mainly in May and June and then again in September and October although smaller hatches do occur throughout the summer. It is unusual in that it seems to hatch more prolifically in bad weather and so many duns are trapped on the water surface unable to get airborne. Hatches can be fairly dense and both sexes are very similar in appearance. Once mating has taken place the female spinner, often referred to as the 'Little Claret Spinner', returns to the water and crawls beneath its surface to lay her eggs. Many spent females get trapped beneath the surface film and are taken by feeding trout.

Size:	Nymph: 8–10mm. Adult: 6–8mm
Distribution:	Widespread except S.E. England
Habitat:	*B. Niger* water with dense weed and other species. Fast stony rivers
Hatch:	Daytime
Season:	April – November, more prolific May – June, Sept – October
Description:	Nymph: Very dark olive Dun: Dark brown-olive body, dull grey-blue wings, yellow-green eyes. Male: dark grey-brown body, dull grey-blue wings, reddish eyes. Small oval spurred hindwings, two tails Spinner: Dark claret-brown body, transparent wings, 'Little Claret Spinner'. Male: white body, last three segments dark orange, black thorax, two long tails, clear wings, 'Jenny Spinner'

Medium Olive (*Baetis Vernus, Tenax, Buceratus*)

Of the early summer flies the Medium Olive is probably one of the most important. Nymphs that are to be found amongst weed beds or moving about amongst bottom debris are very agile swimmers. They have slender bodies with three tails, the middle one being shorter than the other two. These tails are covered with fringes of hairs and it is by means of these that rapid movement is achieved.

Hatches, which occur in the main during May and June, start in late morning until early afternoon. Male and female duns are very similar in appearance with the male being slightly smaller. From mid-afternoon on until dusk male spinners may be seen swarming along the banksides. Fertilized females, commonly called 'Red Spinners', crawl down protruding objects in order to lay their eggs under water. At this time many end up on the surface and so provide a meal for feeding trout.

Size:	Nymph: 10mm. Adult: 6–9mm
Distribution:	Widespread
Habitat:	*Vernus* prefers chalky waters, *Tenax* more acid waters
Hatch:	Late morning, early afternoon
Season:	Mainly May and June but also April and August
Description:	Nymph: Slender body mottled yellow-olive, three tails Dun: Female: brown-olive body, dull grey wings. Male: Grey-olive body, dull grey wings, reddish-brown eyes, two tails Spinner: Female: red-brown body, transparent wings with light brown veins. Male: dark red-brown body, transparent wings, reddish-brown eyes

1. Medium Olive Dun

DRESSING

Hook length: 8–10mm
Thread: Brown
Tail: Blue-dun cock hackle fibres
Abdomen: Hare's ear fur
Rib: Fine gold wire
Wing: Bunch of grey Magic Spinner wing fibres upright
Hackle: Greenwell cock

2. Olive Dun

DRESSING

Hook length: 10–12mm
Thread: Olive
Tail: Olive dun hackle fibres
Abdomen: Medium olive seal's fur sub
Rib: Fine copper wire
Wing: Starling feathers
Hackle: Olive cock

3. Medium Olive Dun

DRESSING

Hook length: 8–12mm
Thread: Black
Tails: Plymouth Rock fibres
Abdomen: Rabbit's fur
Hackle: Plymouth Rock cock

4. Lunn's Particular

DRESSING

Hook length: 10–12mm
Thread: Crimson
Tail: Rhode Island Red hackle fibres
Abdomen: Undyed Rhode Island Red hackle stalk
Thorax: Brown Antron
Wing: Cream poly yarn

5. U.S.D. Polyspinner

DRESSING

Hook length: 10–12mm
Thread: Brown
Tail: Three spaced Magic Spinner fibres
Abdomen: Fly-Rite #5 Rust dubbing
Wing: Clear polythene lightly pierced with a needle
Hackle: Light red game tied in parachute

6. Kite's Imperial

DRESSING

Hook length: 10–12mm
Thread: Purple
Tail: Grey or brown hackle fibres
Abdomen: Natural heron herl
Rib: Fine gold wire
Thorax: Natural heron doubled
Hackle: Honey-dun cock

7. Pheasant-Tail Spinner

DRESSING

Hook length: 10–12mm
Thread: Brown
Tail: Blue-dun hackle fibres
Abdomen: Cock-pheasant tail fibres
Wing: Light blue-dun cock hackle points spent
Hackle: Golden-dun cock

8. Large Dark Olive Dun

DRESSING

Hook length: 10mm
Thread: Olive
Tail: Light blue-dun hackle fibres
Abdomen: Layers of tying thread covered with dark grey-olive dyed moose-mane hair
Wings: Pair of pale starling primary slips
Hackle: Medium-olive cock

9. Houghton Ruby

DRESSING

Hook length: 10mm
Thread: Crimson
Tail: Three white cock hackle fibres
Abdomen: Rhode Island Red hackle stalk dyed crimson
Wing: Two light blue-dun hackle tips tied spent
Hackle: Rhode Island Red cock

10. Iron Blue Dun

DRESSING

Hook length: 8–10mm
Thread: Crimson
Tail: White cock fibres
Tip: Crimson thread
Abdomen: Dark heron herl
Wing: Shaped dark-dun hackles
Hackle: Dark-dun cock

11. Iron Blue Dun

DRESSING

Hook length: 8–10mm
Thread: Crimson
Tail: Dark slate-blue cock hackle fibres
Tip: Crimson thread
Abdomen: Dark heron herl
Hackle: Dark slate-blue cock palmered halfway down abdomen

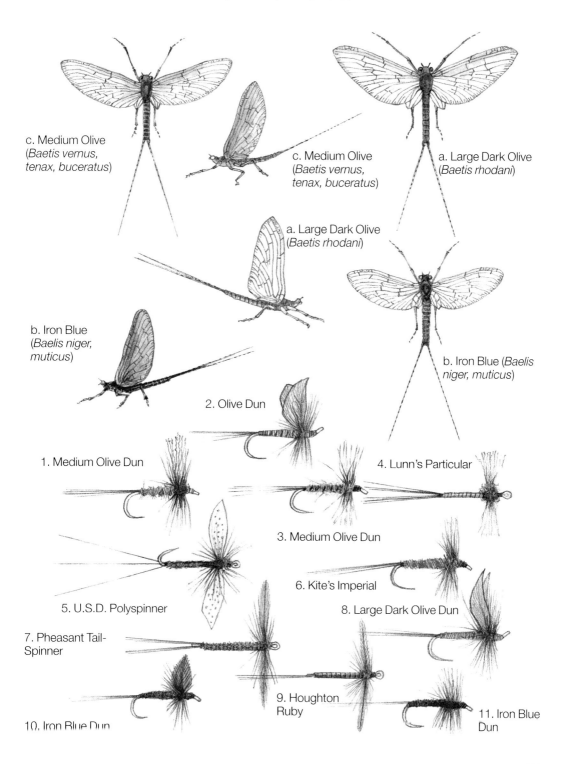

c. Medium Olive (*Baetis vernus, tenax, buceratus*)

c. Medium Olive (*Baetis vernus, tenax, buceratus*)

a. Large Dark Olive (*Baetis rhodani*)

a. Large Dark Olive (*Baetis rhodani*)

b. Iron Blue (*Baelis niger, muticus*)

b. Iron Blue (*Baelis niger, muticus*)

2. Olive Dun

1. Medium Olive Dun

4. Lunn's Particular

3. Medium Olive Dun

5. U.S.D. Polyspinner

6. Kite's Imperial

7. Pheasant Tail-Spinner

8. Large Dark Olive Dun

9. Houghton Ruby

10. Iron Blue Dun

11. Iron Blue Dun

81

Dark Olive, Large Green Dun, Turkey Brown (Adult) 4

Dark Olive (*Baetis Atrebatinus*)

This is an uncommon species that is occasionally found on chalkstreams and calcareous rivers in Yorkshire. The nymph is of the agile darter type inhabiting weed beds and sometimes found moving rapidly about on the river bed. Male and female duns have two tails and tiny oval hindwings and are very similar in appearance, as are male and female spinners.

Size:	Nymph: 10–12mm Adult: 8–10mm
Distribution:	Uncommon
Habitat:	Chalkstreams
Hatch:	Daytime
Season:	April – June and September – October
Description:	Nymph: Agile darter nymph, brown-olive in colour Dun: Female: dark olive body, grey wings, dark greenish-olive eyes. Male: dark olive body, grey wings, pale red-brown eyes Spinner: Female: dark red-brown with paler bands, transparent wings. Male: pale grey-green body, last three segments amber, transparent wings

Large Green Dun (*Ecdyonurus Insignis*)

This again is a less common fly being localized to the North, South Wales and the West Country. It is found on fast-flowing rivers and streams with stony beds and slightly chalky water. The nymph, one of the stone clinging type, is broad and flat-bodied with strong feet for gripping in the strong currents. Adults may be seen on the wing throughout the summer although hatches are sparse.

Both male and female dun are similar in appearance. Spinners are also very much alike and have distinct dark patches on the leading edge of the forewings. The male has unusually long tails.

Size:	Nymph: 15mm. Adult: 12mm
Distribution:	Localized in the North, South Wales and the West Country
Habitat:	Fast-flowing water
Hatch:	Afternoon
Season:	May – September, especially July and August
Description:	Nymph: Grey-brown flat stone-clinger type nymph Dun: Medium olive body with brown segmentation, fawn wings with heavy brown veining, greenish-brown eyes. Male same as female but darker body Spinner: Olive-green body, transparent wings heavily veined, distinctive dark patch on leading edge. Male same as female but longer tails

Turkey Brown (*Paraleptophlebia Submarginata*)

An uncommon fly, localized to parts of the West Country, Wales and Northern England. The Turkey Brown is found only on slow-flowing stretches of water. The nymph, a laboured swimmer, spends its life hiding amongst the thicker weeds and bottom debris. Duns, which hatch at the surface during daytime, are rather sparse and it is unusual to see any number on the water together at the same time. Spinners are an uncommon sight on the water in daytime and so are of little significance to the angler.

Size: Nymph: 15mm.
Adult: 12mm
Distribution: Uncommon
Habitat: Slower flowing water
Hatch: Daytime
Season: May and June
Description: Nymph: laboured swimmer type, yellowish-olive-brown
Dun: Dark blackish-brown body, fawn mottled wings, black eyes, clear patch in central forewings. Male same as female but dull red eyes. Spinner: Dark brown body ringed with pale brown segmentation, transparent wings with pale brown veining. Male: brown body ringed with cream, last three segments dark brown, transparent wings, pale brown leading edge, dark red eyes, oval brown mark on underside of each body segment

1. Dark Olive Dun

DRESSING

Hook length: 10mm
Thread: Olive
Tail: Dark olive dyed cock fibres
Abdomen: Dark olive dubbed wool
Rib: Electron-white fluorescent floss
Hackle: Slate-blue and brown-olive cock hackles wound together

2. No Hackle Dun

DRESSING

Hook length: 10–12mm
Thread: Brown
Tail: Two bunches of cream cock fibres separated by a ball of dubbing
Abdomen: Olive Fly-Rite #10
Thorax: Dark tan #20
Wing: Two grey duck wing quill slips

3. U.S.D. Paradun 2

DRESSING

Hook length: 10–12mm
Thread: Black
Tail: Honey or light ginger hackle fibres with black tips
Abdomen: Hare's ear fur
Wing: Grey goose slips
Hackle: Greenwell or Ginger with black tips wound parachute style. The fly is tied upside down

4. Loop-Wing Dun

DRESSING

Hook length: 10–12mm
Thread: Brown
Tail: Mallard flank fibres dyed olive
Abdomen: Mallard flank fibres dyed olive
Rib: Brown thread
Wings: Body fibres looped and parted into two wings
Hackle: Greenwell cock

5. Dark Olive Spinner

DRESSING

Hook length: 10–12mm
Thread: Olive
Tail: Light olive hackle fibres or microfibetts
Abdomen: An underbody of a single layer of copper wire covered with mix of olive and rust seal's fur sub
Rib: Fine gold wire
Wing: Clear Antron poly wing fibres

6. Large Green Dun

DRESSING

Hook length: 12–15mm
Thread: Dark brown
Tail: Dark dun cock fibres
Abdomen: Green-grey seal's fur sub
Rib: Dark brown thread
Hackle: Cock dyed green with a grizzle dyed green in front

7. Pheasant Tail Spinner

DRESSING

Hook length: 12–15mm
Thread: Orange
Tail: Honey-dun cock fibres
Abdomen: Centre cock pheasant tail fibres
Hackle: Rusty or sandy-dun cock trimmed top and bottom spent

8. Large Green Spinner

DRESSING

Hook length: 12mm
Thread: Green
Tail: Dark-dun cock hackle fibres
Abdomen: Stripped peacock quill dyed green
Wings: Grizzle cock hackle tips tied spent
Hackle: Cock hackle dyed green

9. Turkey Brown

DRESSING

Hook length: 12mm
Thread: Yellow
Tail: Cree cock hackle fibres
Abdomen: Hare's ear fur
Rib: Yellow thread
Hackles: Short red game with cree hackle in front

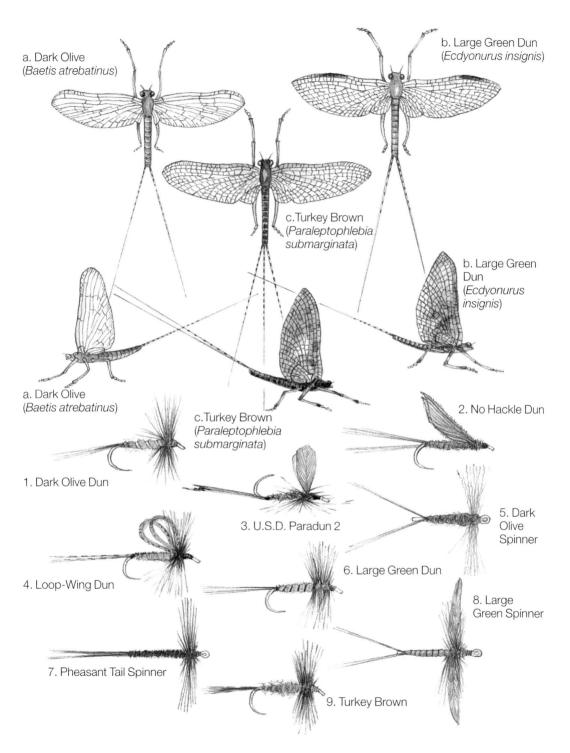

a. Dark Olive
(*Baetis atrebatinus*)

b. Large Green Dun
(*Ecdyonurus insignis*)

c.Turkey Brown
(*Paraleptophlebia submarginata*)

b. Large Green Dun
(*Ecdyonurus insignis*)

a. Dark Olive
(*Baetis atrebatinus*)

c.Turkey Brown
(*Paraleptophlebia submarginata*)

2. No Hackle Dun

1. Dark Olive Dun

3. U.S.D. Paradun 2

5. Dark Olive Spinner

4. Loop-Wing Dun

6. Large Green Dun

8. Large Green Spinner

7. Pheasant Tail Spinner

9. Turkey Brown

Small Spurwing, Large Spurwing, Pale Evening Dun (Adult) 5

Small Spurwing (*Centroptilum Luteolum*)

The small spurwing was one of the flies classed as Pale Wateries and had the name 'Small Sky Blue'. It is a fly usually found on fast to medium flowing rivers but can also be present in large numbers on some lakes. It is a very common species that is present throughout the summer and even into early autumn. The nymph is an agile darter present in large numbers in weed beds, especially those of chalk and limestone waters.

Hatches take place throughout the day and are on a very large scale, although on upland lakes and rocky streams they are not as prolific as elsewhere. Both the male and female spinner are important to the angler as males swarm over the margins and mating actually takes place over the water. Many spent females also end up on the surface as they fly over the water, dipping down into it occasionally to lay their eggs.

Size:	Nymph: 8mm.
	Adult: 6–8mm
Distribution:	Widespread and common
Habitat:	Most rivers and some lakes
Hatch:	Daytime
Season:	May and September
Description:	Nymph: Agile darter type, pale olive-brown in colour
	Dun: Pale olive-grey body, pale grey wings, pale green eyes. Male same as female, orange-red eyes. Hindwings have pronounced spur.
	Spinner: Yellow-amber body, transparent wings faint olive veining, known as 'Little Amber Spinner'.
	Male: Whitish body, last three segments pale orange-brown, transparent wings, orange-red eyes

Large Spurwing (*Centroptilum Pennulatum*)

This is a rather uncommon fly being localized in the north and southern parts of England. It has a preference for lowland rivers and streams with slow to medium-flowing stretches. The nymph lives amongst bottom debris and weed beds and is of the agile darter type.

Adults, which only hatch in small numbers, are present from late May to early autumn. Male flies do not swarm until late afternoon and rarely end up on the surface of the water so are of little importance. After laying the eggs on the water, spent females frequently fall to the surface.

Size:	Nymph: 10mm.
	Adult: 8–10mm
Distribution:	Localized and uncommon
Habitat:	Slower flowing stretches of lowland rivers and streams
Hatch:	Afternoon
Season:	May – October
Description:	Nymph: Agile darter type nymph, dark olive-brown
	Dun: Pale olive-grey body, blue-grey wings, yellow-green eyes.
	Male: pale olive-brown body, last three segments amber, blue-grey wings, orange eyes.
	Spinner: Rich amber body, grey segmentation, transparent wings, known as 'Large Amber Spinner'.
	Male: translucent white body with pale red ringing, last three segments are dark amber with transparent wings and orange eyes

Pale Evening Dun (*Procloeon Pseudorufulum*)

This widespread, but localized, fly is usually seen on medium to slow flowing rivers and is fairly common on our chalkstreams. Adult flies are quite easily recognised as, apart from the Pond Olive, it is the only river fly with no hindwings.

A further distinguishing feature of the male is that, along with the Pale Watery, it is the only adult with yellow eyes. Duns normally hatch sporadically towards dusk, often in substantial numbers. It would seem that females possibly lay their eggs very late into the evening which would help to explain why they are seldom seen on the water.

Size: Nymph: 6–8mm.
Adult: 4–6mm
Distribution: Widespread but localized
Habitat: Medium to slow flowing water
Hatch: Evening
Season: May – August
Description: Nymph: dark mottled olive
Dun: pale straw body tinged with red-brown, pale grey wings. Male: straw coloured body tinged with pale brown, pale grey wings, yellow eyes. Spinner: pale golden olive-brown body, transparent wings. Male: greyish-white body, last three segments amber-orange, transparent wings, pale yellow eyes

1. Small Spurwing Dun

DRESSING

Hook length: 6–8mm
Thread: Pale yellow
Tail: Cream cock hackle fibres
Abdomen: Cream and pale olive seal's fur sub (3:1)
Hackle: Cream cock or blue-dun cock

2. Large Spurwing Dun

DRESSING

Hook length: 8–10mm
Thread: Cream
Tail: Cream cock fibres
Abdomen: Olive-grey seal's fur sub
Wing: Grey polypropylene yarn
Hackle: Pale olive cock

3. Large Spurwing Spinner

DRESSING

Hook length: 8–10mm
Thread: Orange
Tail: Pale blue-dun fibres
Abdomen: Amber and cream seal's fur sub (1:2)
Wing: White polypropylene yarn tied spent

4. Little Marryat

DRESSING

Hook length: 8–10mm
Thread: White
Tail: Cream dun cock fibres
Abdomen: Pale coffee-coloured seal's fur sub
Wing: Pale starling or bunched feather fibres
Hackle: Cream-coloured dun cock

5. Ginger Quill

Hook length: 8–10mm
Thread: Brown
Tail: Ginger cock fibres
Abdomen: Natural peacock eye quill
Wing: Pale blue-dun hackle tips or starling
Hackle: Ginger cock

6. Small Spurwing Spinner

Hook length: 6–8mm
Thread: Hot orange
Tail: Cream cock fibres
Abdomen: Tip of orange thread cream (Fly-Rite #25) poly dubbing
Hackle: White or cream cock tied parachute

7. Itchen Olive

Hook length: 10mm
Thread: Primrose
Tail: Pale grey hackle fibres
Abdomen: Medium grey seal's fur sub
Rib: Primrose thread
Hackle: Light grey cock

8. Pale Evening Dun

Hook length: 6–8mm
Thread: White
Tail: Cream cock fibres
Abdomen: Grey goose herls doubled at thorax
Hackle: Cream cock

9. Pale Evening Dun

Hook length: 6–8mm
Thread: Yellow
Tail: Cream cock fibres
Abdomen: Cream Fly-Rite #25 poly dubbing
Wing: Light grey poly yarn set upright
Hackle: Cream cock

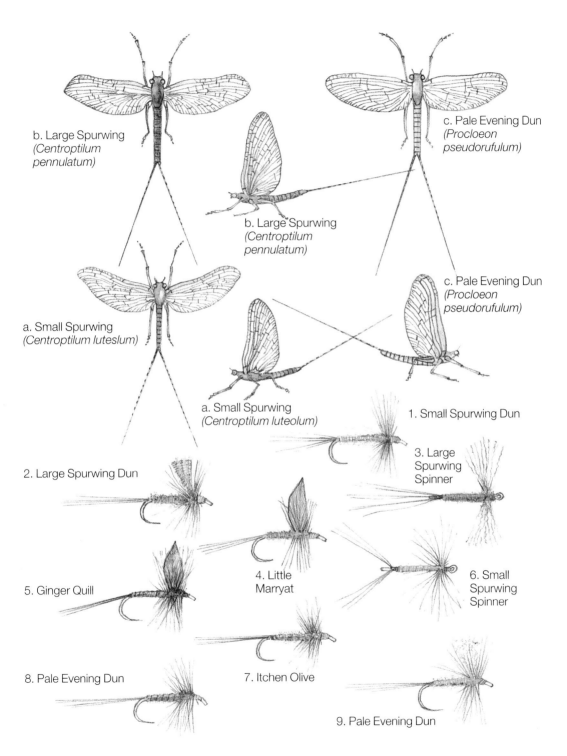

b. Large Spurwing
*(Centroptilum
pennulatum)*

c. Pale Evening Dun
*(Procloeon
pseudorufulum)*

b. Large Spurwing
*(Centroptilum
pennulatum)*

a. Small Spurwing
(Centroptilum luteslum)

c. Pale Evening Dun
*(Procloeon
pseudorufulum)*

a. Small Spurwing
(Centroptilum luteolum)

1. Small Spurwing Dun

3. Large
Spurwing
Spinner

2. Large Spurwing Dun

4. Little
Marryat

6. Small
Spurwing
Spinner

5. Ginger Quill

8. Pale Evening Dun

7. Itchen Olive

9. Pale Evening Dun

Claret Dun, Sepia Dun, Dusky Yellowstreak (Adult) 6

Claret Dun (*Leptophlebia Vespertina*)

This is mainly a stillwater fly, although there is some occurrence on small upland streams of a moderately acid nature. The nymph, which has a slightly flattened, reddish-brown body and three very long tails, is a laboured swimmer and only leaves the riverbed to emerge. This usually takes place near the margins in open water from early afternoon onwards. Transformation to spinner usually occurs away from the water's edge, but both dun and spinner may be seen on the water at the same time. Adult males swarm around vegetation near the edge but do not very often end up on the water. Females fly over the water, periodically dipping their abdomens to lay eggs, and often fall onto the surface when spent.

Size:	Nymph: 10–12mm. Adult: 10mm
Distribution:	Uncommon and localized
Habitat:	Lakes and small rivers of acid nature
Hatch:	Daytime
Season:	May – July
Description:	Nymph: reddish-brown, three long tails Dun: Dark brown-black body with claret tinge, dark grey forewings, buff hindwings, three tails. Male as for female Spinner: Claret-brown body, transparent wings, light brown veining, three tails. Male as for female

Sepia Dun (*Leptophlebia Marginata*)

The Sepia Dun occupies much the same habitat as the Claret Dun but is probably even more uncommon. Nymphs live in the shallow margins of rivers and lakes and, when emergence is about to take place, crawl up protruding vegetation. Adults are seen on the wing in April and early May. The Sepia Dun is slightly larger than the Claret with a browner body and light brown wings. Spinners are difficult to tell apart except that the Sepia has a smoky area on the forewing's leading edge.

Size:	Nymph: 10–12mm. Adult: 10mm
Distribution:	Uncommon and localized
Habitat:	Lakes and small rivers of acid nature
Hatch:	Daytime
Season:	April and early May
Description:	Nymph: Laboured swimmer type nymph, reddish-brown, three long tails Dun: Dark sepia-brown body, pale fawn-brown wings heavily veined brown, dark brown eyes. Male as female, dark red-brown eyes Spinner: Dark red-brown body, transparent wings veined light brown with smoky patch on leading edge of forewing. Male dark brown body

Dusky Yellowstreak (*Heptagenia Lateralis*)

The Dusky Yellowstreak, formerly called Dark Dun, takes its name because of a distinct yellow streak on each side of the thorax just before the base of the forewing. This streak is present in both dun and spinner. It is a rather localized fly being mainly confined to upland streams and rivers or lakes with stony beds and shores. The nymph is of the stone clinging type. Hatches occur in the late afternoon throughout the summer months, often in considerable numbers. Males only swarm in small groups and often away from the water's edge. Females lay their eggs by dipping their abdomens into the water's surface during flight.

Size: Nymph: 10–12mm.
Adult: 10mm
Distribution: Localized to parts of North Devon, Wales, Scotland, Northern areas and parts of Ireland
Habitat: Mainly upland streams, rivers and lakes with stony beds
Hatch: Dusk

Season: May – September
Description: Nymph: Stone-clinger type, olive-brown, some lighter markings
Dun: Dark greyish-brown body, very dark grey wings, black eyes. Male same as female
Spinner: Brown-olive body, transparent wings with brown leading edge. Yellow streaks on thorax at bottom of wing roots. Male same as female

1. Sepia Dun

DRESSING

Hook length: 10mm
Thread: Dark brown
Tail: Dark brown or black cock fibres
Abdomen: Dark heron herls doubled at thorax
Rib: Fine gold wire
Hackle: Black cock with some brown

2. Sepia Dun

DRESSING

Hook length: 10mm
Thread: Maroon
Tail: Pheasant tail fibres
Abdomen: Pheasant tail fibres
Rib: Fine gold wire
Wing: Mottled brown cock wing-slips or similar
Hackle: Furnace cock

3. Pheasant-Tail Spinner

DRESSING

Hook length: 10mm
Thread: Brown
Tail: Blue-dun hackle fibres
Abdomen: Cock-pheasant tail fibres
Wing: Blue-dun cock hackle points spent
Hackle: Golden-dun cock

4. Dusky Yellowstreak

DRESSING

Hook length: 10mm
Thread: Brown
Tail: Blue-dun cock fibres or Microfibetts
Abdomen: Heron herl
Rib: Brown thread
Hackle: Dark blue-dun and grizzle cocks

5. Claret Dun

Hook length: 10mm
Thread: Claret
Tail: Dark blue-dun cock hackle fibres
Abdomen: Dark heron herl dyed claret
Rib: Fine gold wire
Hackle: Dark blue-dun cut with a V under

6. Claret Dun

Hook length: 10mm
Threat: Claret
Tail: Dark rusty-dun cock hackle fibres
Abdomen: Seal's fur dark claret
Rib: Fine gold wire
Hackle: Dark rusty-dun cock

7. Claret Spinner

Hook length: 10–12mm
Thread: Black
Tail: Badger hackle fibres
Abdomen: Claret seal's fur sub
Wings: Badger cock tied in bunched spent wings

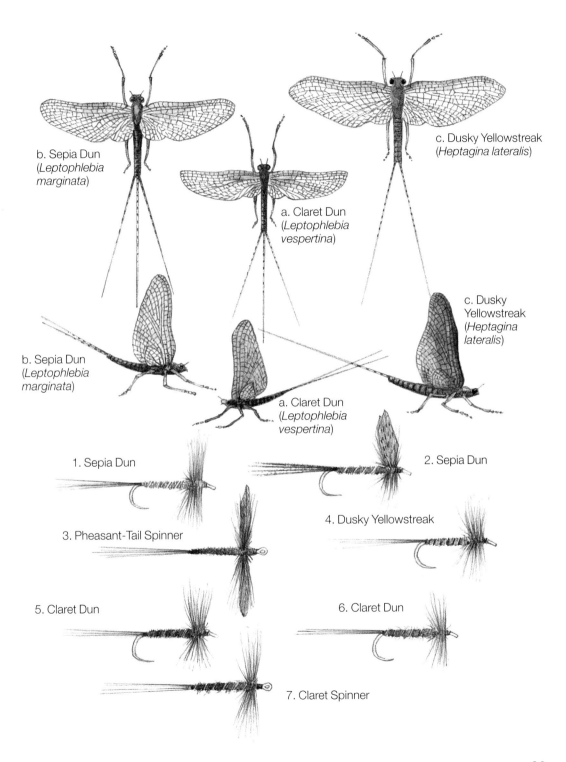

b. Sepia Dun
(*Leptophlebia marginata*)

a. Claret Dun
(*Leptophlebia vespertina*)

c. Dusky Yellowstreak
(*Heptagina lateralis*)

b. Sepia Dun
(*Leptophlebia marginata*)

a. Claret Dun
(*Leptophlebia vespertina*)

c. Dusky Yellowstreak
(*Heptagina lateralis*)

1. Sepia Dun

2. Sepia Dun

3. Pheasant-Tail Spinner

4. Dusky Yellowstreak

5. Claret Dun

6. Claret Dun

7. Claret Spinner

Olive Upright, Large Brook Dun, Pond Olive, Lake Olive (Adult) 7

Olive Upright (*Rithrogena Semicolorata*)

The Olive Upright is a fly common to swift stony rivers and streams throughout Britain. The nymph, which is of the stone clinging type, is greatly affected by the temperature and many suffer an early death on hot days in summer. The actual rate of development is also affected by temperature and so hatching times can vary from year to year. Hatches, which occur late afternoon and early evening, can be quite heavy and cause somewhat of a stir amongst a trout population. The spinner, which has a yellowish tinge to its wings and an ability to ascend vertically in flight, is known as the Yellow Upright. From mid-afternoon onwards, male spinners may be seen swarming over the water and late in the day females can be found crawling down vegetation or on protruding stones, dipping their abdomens into the water to lay eggs.

Size:	Nymph: 10–12mm. Adult: 9–12mm
Distribution:	Widespread
Habitat:	Swift-flowing rivers and streams
Hatch:	Late afternoon and early evening
Season:	May – July
Description:	Nymph: Light golden-brown with dark markings, especially on largest leg segment Dun: Grey-olive-brown body, dark blue-grey wings, buff coloured rear edge to hindwing, dull green eyes. Male black-olive eyes Spinner: Dull yellow-olive body, transparent wings veined with pale brown and smoky bronze, dull olive eyes. Male brown-olive body

Large Brook Dun (*Ecdyonorus Torrentis*)

This is a fly of small stony streams and brooks; it is very seldom encountered on our large rivers. Although quite common, except for the South and East of England, it can be localized in the areas where it is found. The nymph, with its flat sturdy body, is well adapted for the swift currents in which it lives. Adults are on the wing from late March to early July and can easily be confused with others of the *Ecdyonorus* species. Two distinguishing features are the dark diagonal bands on the side of the body and the yellowish leading edge to the forewing. Hatches are often sparse but can occur throughout the day. Females lay from early afternoon onwards, flying over the surface and occasionally dipping their abdomens to release the eggs. Males, which have unusually long tails, often swarm far from the water so have little significance for the angler.

Size:	Nymph: 14–16mm. Adult: 10–16mm
Distribution:	Localized but common
Habitat:	Stony streams and brooks
Hatch:	Daytime
Season:	March – July
Description:	Nymph: Flat sturdy body, yellow-olive to red-brown Dun: Drab olive-brown with darker brown diagonal bands along sides, pale fawn dark brown veining mottled with yellowish leading edge, brown-olive eyes. Male as female Spinner: Dark olive-brown body, darker diagonal bands, transparent veined with black wings and yellowish leading edge, brown eyes. Male brown veined wings, green-black eyes

Pond Olive (*Cloeon Dipterum*)

The Pond Olive is found mainly on small stillwater, but occasionally on stretches of very slow-flowing rivers. The nymph, which spends its life amongst the weed beds, is of the agile darter type. Duns emerge from late morning to early evening in open water usually during June and July. It is possible for a second hatch to occur later in the year so adults may also be seen in September. The dun is very similar in appearance to the Medium Olive but is darker in colour and has black ringed tails. The female spinner is also known as the 'Apricot Spinner' due to its very distinctive coloration. Adult flies have two tails and no hindwings.

Size:	Nymph: 10–12mm. Adult: 8-10mm
Distribution:	Widespread
Habitat:	Stillwaters and some slow-flowing rivers
Hatch:	Daytime
Season:	June – July and September
Description:	Nymph: Agile darter type nymph, olive-brown, brown-grey body
Dun: Brown-olive body, medium-dark grey wings.
Male: Grey-olive body, pale grey wings, orange-brown eyes
Spinner: Apricot body, red tinged transparent wings, yellow-olive leading edge.
Male: Dull cream body, last three segments brown, transparent wings, brown leading edge, orange-red eyes

Lake Olive (*Cloeon Simile*) (not pictured)

The Lake Olive is very similar to the Pond Olive although it is slightly duller in colour and is usually found in larger lakes. For angling purposes, all patterns relating to the Pond Olive will be suitable for the Lake Olive.

1. Olive Upright Dun

DRESSING

Hook length: 10–12mm
Thread: Dark green
Tail: Medium olive cock hackle fibres
Abdomen: Peacock quill dyed olive
Hackle: Medium olive cock

2. Mole Fly

DRESSING

Hook length: 10–12mm
Thread: Dark olive
Abdomen: Dark olive thread
Rib: Fine gold wire
Wings: Mottled hen pheasant tied forward
Hackle: Furnace tied length of abdomen and full at eye

3. Pheasant Tail Spinner

DRESSING

Hook length: 10–12mm
Thread: Hot orange
Tail: Honey-dun cock fibres
Abdomen: Cock-pheasant tail fibres
Hackle: Rusty dun cut top and bottom spent

4. March Brown

DRESSING

Hook length: 10–12mm
Thread: Yellow
Tail: Cree cock hackle fibres
Abdomen: Hare's ear fur mixed yellow seal's fur sub
Rib: Yellow thread
Wing: Pheasant wing quill
Hackle: Cree cock hackle

5. Olive Quill

DRESSING

Hook length: 10–12mm
Thread: Pale yellow
Tail: Medium olive cock fibres
Abdomen: Peacock quill dyed olive
Wing: Starling wing
Hackle: Medium olive cock

6. Red Spinner

DRESSING

Hook length: 10–12mm
Thread: Red-orange
Tail: Red cock hackle fibres
Abdomen: Red seal's fur sub
Rib: Fine gold wire
Wing: Blue-dun cock hackle tips tied spent

7. Pond Olive Spinner

DRESSING

Hook length: 8–10mm
Thread: Orange
Tail: Badger cock fibres
Abdomen: Condor herl dyed apricot, covered with p.v.c.
Wing: Blue-dun hackle tips spent
Hackle: Honey-dun fibres tied under each wing

8. Pond Olive Dun

DRESSING

Hook length: 8–10mm
Thread: Olive
Tail: Blue-dun fibres
Abdomen: Goose herl dyed olive
Rib: Olive-brown thread
Wing: Blue-dun hackle fibres
Hackle: Olive cock

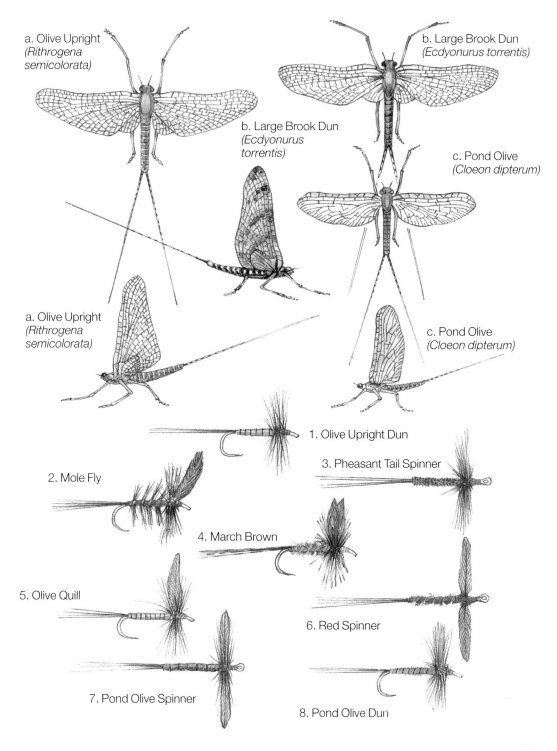

a. Olive Upright
*(Rithrogena
semicolorata)*

b. Large Brook Dun
(Ecdyonurus torrentis)

b. Large Brook Dun
*(Ecdyonurus
torrentis)*

c. Pond Olive
(Cloeon dipterum)

a. Olive Upright
*(Rithrogena
semicolorata)*

c. Pond Olive
(Cloeon dipterum)

1. Olive Upright Dun

2. Mole Fly

3. Pheasant Tail Spinner

4. March Brown

5. Olive Quill

6. Red Spinner

7. Pond Olive Spinner

8. Pond Olive Dun

97

Late March Brown, March Brown, Purple Dun (Adult) 8

Late March Brown (*Ecdyonurus Venosus*)

This uncommon fly, localized to certain parts of the country, is found on fast, stony rivers. The nymph, an algal feeder, spends its life clinging to rocks and stones on the riverbed. As they mature, nymphs move away from the middle of the river and live at the edges, and it is here that they crawl out onto exposed stones for emergence into adult flies. Hatches, although sparse, take place throughout the day and adults may be seen on the wing from March to July. Occasionally a second hatch will take place and adults may be present during August and September. Although similar to the March Brown the absence of a pale central area in the forewings does distinguish the two.

Size:	Nymph: 12–14mm. Adult 10–14mm
Distribution:	Localized to parts of Wales, the North and West Country
Habitat:	Fast, stony rivers
Hatch:	Daytime
Season:	May – July
Description:	Nymph: Stone-clinger nymph, dark brown body with lighter markings Dun: Dull brown body, brown mottled wings. Male as female Spinner: Mahogany-red body, transparent wings, brown veining. Male as female

March Brown (*Rithrogena Haarupi (Germanica)*)

Distribution of the March Brown can be rather localized and somewhat patchy. It is an inhabitant of the faster-flowing northern and western rivers with very stony beds. Main hatches of the fly occur during March and early April. Emergence is in batches, often in the middle of the day, in open water and it is at this time that many flies are taken before becoming airborne. Although the female spinner deposits her eggs at the water surface this usually occurs late in the day and therefore rarely causes much of a rise in the trout population.

Size:	Nymph: 14mm. Adult: 10–14mm
Distribution:	Localized – Wales, the West Country, Northern England and Scotland
Habitat:	Fast, stony rivers
Hatch:	Usually middle of the day
Season:	March – April
Description:	Nymph: Stone-clinger nymph, dark purple-brown-dark brown with some markings. Dun: Dull brown body, straw segmentation, pale fawn wings, dark brown veining with clear patch in central forewing. Male as female Spinner: Dark red-brown segmented straw colour, wings transparent, dark brown veining, distinct brown streak in the middle of each top leg section. Male as female

Purple Dun (*Paraleptophlebia Cincta*)

The Purple Dun is a localized fly to Wales, the West Country and parts of Northern England. It is to be found on fast, stony streams where the nymph, a laboured swimmer, is to be found amongst stones and marginal plants. Hatches, which are rather sparse, take place from mid-morning to late afternoon and adult flies may be present from May through to

August. Adult male spinners may be seen swarming over the water from noon onwards. The female lays her eggs at, or after, dusk.

Size: Nymph: 10mm.
Adult: 8mm
Distribution: Localized – Wales, the West Country and Northern England
Habitat: Fast-flowing streams and rivers
Hatch: Daytime
Season: May – August

Description: Nymph: laboured swimmer, olive-dark brown in colour
Dun: Dark brown tinged purple, blackish-grey wings. Male as female
Spinner: Brown tinged purple, transparent wings with faint brown veining. Male translucent white, last three segments purple-brown, transparent wings, with faint brown veining

1. Purple Bumble

DRESSING

Hook length: 10–12mm
Thread: Purple
Hackle: Palmered blue-dun

2. No-Hackle Dun

DRESSING

Hook length: 10–12mm
Thread: Purple
Tail: Slate-grey hackle fibres
Abdomen: Hare's fur, dark brown
Rib: Purple silk thread
Hackle: Dark grey duck wing sections

3. Great Red Spinner

DRESSING

Hook length: 12mm
Thread: Red
Tail: Natural red cock fibres
Abdomen: Red seal's fur sub
Rib: Fine gold wire
Wing: Blue-dun cock hackle tips tied spent
Hackle: Natural red cock

4. March Brown Dun

DRESSING

Hook length: 10–12mm
Thread: Purple
Tail: Brown partridge breast fibres
Abdomen: Hare's ear
Hackle: Honey cock brown partridge breast feather in front

5. March Brown Dun

DRESSING

Hook length: 10–12mm
Thread: Primrose
Tail: Cree hackle fibres
Abdomen: Mixed hare's ear and yellow seal's fur sub
Rib: Primrose thread
Wing: Dark hen-pheasant quill slips
Hackle: Cree cock

6. Great Red Spinner

DRESSING

Hook length: 12mm
Thread: Claret
Tail: Dark rusty-dun cock fibres
Abdomen: Claret seal's fur sub
Rib: Fine gold wire
Hackle: Rusty-dun cock tied half spent

7. March Brown

DRESSING

Hook length: 10–12mm
Thread: Brown
Tail: Brown cock hackle fibres
Abdomen: Brown and grey hare fur
Wing: Hen pheasant quill slips
Hackle: Brown cock

8. Cinnamon Quill

DRESSING

Hook length: 10–12mm
Thread: Sherry Spinner
Tail: Ginger cock hackle fibres
Abdomen: Pale cinnamon quill
Hackle: Ginger cock ties spent

9. March Brown

DRESSING

Hook length: 10–12mm
Thread: Orange
Tail: Cock pheasant tail fibres
Abdomen: Hare's ear fur
Rib: Fine gold wire
Thorax: Sepia seal's fur sub
Wing: Dark partridge feather fibres
Hackle: Dark red cock

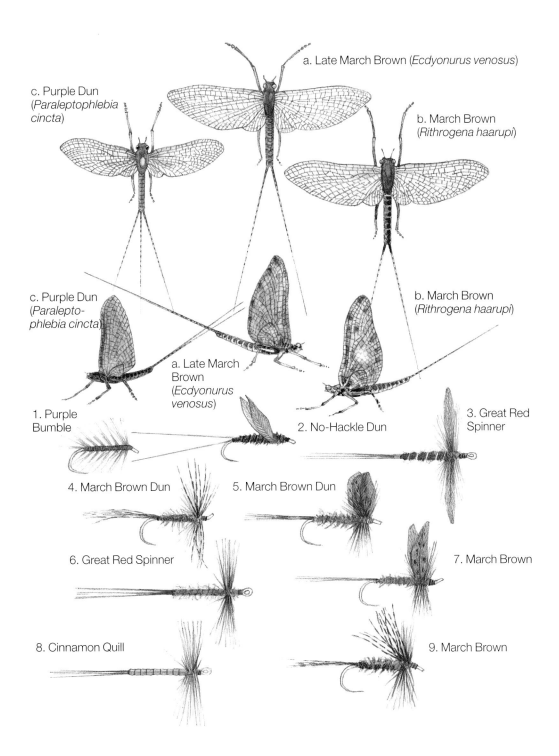

a. Late March Brown (*Ecdyonurus venosus*)

c. Purple Dun (*Paraleptophlebia cincta*)

b. March Brown (*Rithrogena haarupi*)

c. Purple Dun (*Paralepto-phlebia cincta*)

a. Late March Brown (*Ecdyonurus venosus*)

b. March Brown (*Rithrogena haarupi*)

1. Purple Bumble

2. No-Hackle Dun

3. Great Red Spinner

4. March Brown Dun

5. March Brown Dun

6. Great Red Spinner

7. March Brown

8. Cinnamon Quill

9. March Brown

101

12 Miscellaneous

Miscellaneous 1

Ants (*Hymenoptera*)

Ants are mostly of interest to the fly fisherman in the winged stage. The period of ant flights usually occurs on calm, hot days in July and August. These flights usually take place over a few days only, but at times ants can be found on the water in large numbers. As these ants are coloured either black or red, a fly in each colour may prove a worthwhile addition to the fly box.

Greenfly (*Aphis*)

Aphis are found in such great numbers on vegetation throughout the summer, many thousands must fall or be flown onto the water and are often eagerly taken by trout.

Wasps and Bees (*Hymenoptera*)

Although of very little value to the fisherman, trout will take them when they are occasionally blown or fall onto the water.

Caterpillars

In summer caterpillars from trees and waterside vegetation may fall or be blown onto the water surface and be consumed by trout, mostly lying close into the bankside or under trees.

Reed Smuts (*Similium*)

These small, flat-winged flies inhabit rivers and stillwaters. They are mostly coloured dark brown or black with transparent wings. The larvae live amongst the weeds then change into pupae, rising to the surface to hatch into the adult fly. The trout will take them at any stage.

Lacewings (*Planipenna*)

The Lacewing has a green body and pale green transparent wings. It is common throughout the summer but of very little importance to the fly fisherman.

Moths (*Lepidoptera*)

Moths are found on the water occasionally and mostly at dusk. Although there is a family of moths that are aquatic, they are mostly very similar to the terrestrial moths so a pattern in white and brown will suffice. As they are also quite similar to sedges in their movements and shape, a sedge.pattern will suffice.

Grasshopper (*Orthoptera*)

Occasionally grasshoppers will make a mistake and jump onto the water and trout will take them but this must be on such rare occasions that carrying the artificial might seem quite superfluous.

Miscellaneous 1

1. Black Ant

DRESSING

Hook length: 4–7mm
Thread: Black
Abdomen: Black polypropylene tied fatter front and back to represent body and head
Hackle: Black cock

2. McMurray Ant

DRESSING

Hook length: 4–7mm
Thread: Black
Abdomen: Two small cylinders of balsa wood fixed to the hook shank with nylon mono and varnished black or red
Hackle: Black cock or natural red cock wound in the middle of the two balsa cylinders

3. Black or Brown Ant

DRESSING

Hook length: 4–7mm
Thread: Black or brown
Abdomen: Two small shaped pieces of cork at each end of hook shank, split and glued on
Wing: Two white cock hackle tips tied in behind front piece of cork
Hackle: Black or brown cock hackle wound over wing roots

4. Super Ant

DRESSING

Hook length: 4–7mm
Thread: Black
Abdomen: Black plastazote polyethylene foam shaped to body and head
Legs: Black polypropylene monofilament

5. Aphis

DRESSING

Hook length: 4–6mm
Thread: Pale green
Tail: Short blue-dun cock
Abdomen: Light green floss
Hackle: Blue-dun cock

6. Para Aphis

DRESSING

Hook length: 4–6mm
Thread: Pale green
Abdomen: Pale Green thread tied fat
Hackle: Badger cock very short tied parachute

7. Greenfly

DRESSING

Hook length: 4–6mm
Thread: Pale green
Abdomen: Pale green thread tied fat
Wing: White poly yarn
Hackle: Badger cock very short

8. Wasp Grub

DRESSING

Hook length: 14mm
Thread: Brown
Abdomen: Dark brown seal's fur sub mixed with black
Rib: Thick yellow thread
Wing: Grey mallard tied flat over the back
Hackle: Black cock

9. Bee

DRESSING

Hook length: 14mm
Thread: Black
Abdomen: Brown banded yellow or black seal's fur sub
Wing: Partridge or hen-pheasant tied flat over back
Hackle: Furnace cock

10. White Ermine Moth

DRESSING

Hook length: 16mm
Thread: Black
Tail: Orange wool
Abdomen: Dubbed white fur or wool
Rib: Black thread
Hackle: Grey partridge

11. Skittering Moth

DRESSING

Hook length: 16mm (Swedish Dry Fly hook)
Thread: White
Abdomen: Dubbed natural white fur
Wing: White elk or deer hair
Hackle: Cream or white cock

12. Coachman

DRESSING

Hook length: 14mm
Thread: Brown
Abdomen: Bronze peacock herl
Wing: White duck
Hackle: Natural red cock

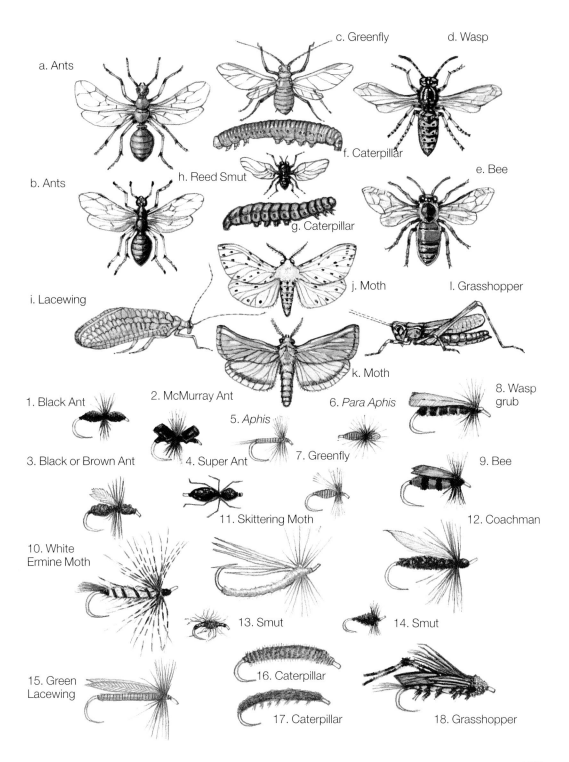

a. Ants

c. Greenfly

d. Wasp

b. Ants

h. Reed Smut

f. Caterpillar

e. Bee

g. Caterpillar

i. Lacewing

j. Moth

l. Grasshopper

k. Moth

1. Black Ant

2. McMurray Ant

5. *Aphis*

6. *Para Aphis*

8. Wasp grub

3. Black or Brown Ant

4. Super Ant

7. Greenfly

9. Bee

11. Skittering Moth

12. Coachman

10. White Ermine Moth

13. Smut

14. Smut

15. Green Lacewing

16. Caterpillar

17. Caterpillar

18. Grasshopper

13. Smut

DRESSING

Hook length: 3–6mm
Thread: Brown
Abdomen: Blood-red cow's hair over thin copper wire with four turns of silver wire at either end of body, the cow's hair is picked out and soaked in silicone liquid to trap air bubbles

14. Smut

DRESSING

Hook length: 3–6mm
Thread: Black
Abdomen: Black ostrich herl shaped fatter towards eye
Hackle: Short-fibred black cock

15. Green Lacewing

DRESSING

Hook length: 14mm
Thread: Bright green
Abdomen: Bright green floss
Wing: Two pale blue-dun hackles tied over the body
Hackle: Dyed green cock

16. Caterpillar

DRESSING

Hook length: 14–16mm
Thread: Green
Abdomen: Green ostrich herl
Rib: Green thread

17. Caterpillar

DRESSING

Hook length: 14–16mm
Thread: Brown
Abdomen: Brown ostrich herl
Rib: Red game palmered down abdomen and cut very short to body

18. Grasshopper

DRESSING

Hook length: 16mm
Thread: Brown
Tail: Red deer hair
Abdomen: Yellow wool palmered brown cock cut short
Wing: Mottled turkey wing quill
Overwing: Yellow deer hair
Hackle: Natural deer hair
Legs: Two knotted brown grizzle hackle fibres
Head: Deer hair spun and clipped

Miscellaneous 2

Beetles and Larva (*Coleoptera*)

Many kinds of beetles may occasionally be encountered on the water, some because they lead an aquatic life, others because they have accidentally landed on the water's surface. Of the some 4,000 species of British beetles a few are well known to the fisherman, amongst which are the Coch-y-bonddu. This is a small beetle with a metallic green thorax and brown wings.

The larvae of beetles range a great deal in size and colour from the tiny Riffle beetle to the voracious *Dytiscus*, Great Diving beetle larva. Two other well known beetles that are prolific enough to warrant attention from the fisherman are the Soldier and the Sailor beetle. They are about half an inch long, the Soldier beetle with orange-red-brown wings with blue-black tips and a dark yellow body. The Sailor beetle is very similar to the Soldier beetle but with dull blue wings and red-brown body.

Water Boatmen (*Corixae*)

Waterboatmen, which may be found darting around in the shallows and amongst weed beds, often draw the attention of feeding trout and an artificial tying of this insect can often prove worthwhile. They vary in size with legs used like oars, the back is shiny and mostly brown in colour, the underneath is mostly white.

Snails

Although snails mostly live on the river or lake bed and among the weeds, in high summer they rise to the surface and float in the surface film. At this time trout, that are full of snails, can be caught.

Spiders

Many terrestrial spiders are blown from trees and vegetation onto the water surface. Along with aquatic spiders they provide another food source for the hungry trout.

1. Coch-y-bonddhu

DRESSING

Hook length: 8mm
Thread: Black or brown
Tip: Flat gold tinsel
Abdomen: Peacock herl
Hackle: Coch-y-bonddhu

2. Black Beetle

DRESSING

Hook length: 6–8mm
Thread: Black
Abdomen: Black seal's fur sub with a back of varnished black raffene
Hackle: Palmered black cock trimmed over top

3. Eric's Beetle

DRESSING

Hook length: 8mm
Thread: Black
Abdomen: Yellow wool with bronze peacock over leaving yellow tip at bend
Hackle: Black cock

4. Red-Eyed Derby Beetle

DRESSING

Hook length: 8mm
Thread: Black
Abdomen: Bronze peacock herl
Hackle: Black cock
Eyes: Two small red beads

5. Deerhair Beetle

DRESSING

Hook length: 8mm
Thread: Black monocord
Legs: Three strands of girdle bug elastic
Abdomen: Black deer hair formed into a two-part, shaped body and varnished

6. Jansen Beetle

DRESSING

Hook length: 8–10mm
Thread: Black
Abdomen: Fly foam in black or grey shaped and tied over, brown polypropylene dubbing
Legs: Peacock herl tied behind head and clipped to length

7. Sailor Beetle

DRESSING

Hook length: 8–10mm
Thread: Black
Abdomen: Brown floss
Wing Case: Blue-black raffene
Hackle: Black cock

8. Soldier Beetle

DRESSING

Hook length: 8–10mm
Thread: Orange
Abdomen: Red-orange seal's fur
Wing Case: Cock-pheasant breast fibres
Hackle: Red cock

Miscellaneous 2

Beetles and larva a,b,c,d,e,f,g,h

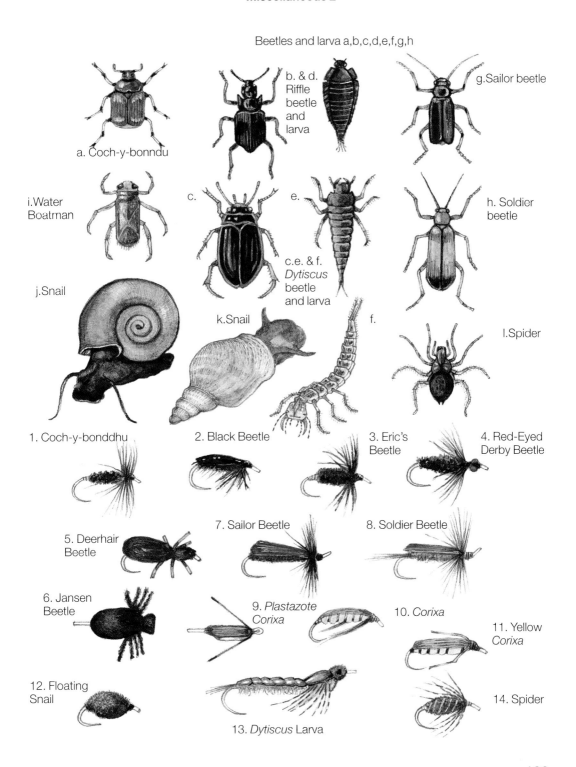

a. Coch-y-bonndu

b. & d. Riffle beetle and larva

g. Sailor beetle

i. Water Boatman

c.

e.

h. Soldier beetle

c.e. & f. *Dytiscus* beetle and larva

j. Snail

k. Snail

f.

l. Spider

1. Coch-y-bonddhu

2. Black Beetle

3. Eric's Beetle

4. Red-Eyed Derby Beetle

5. Deerhair Beetle

7. Sailor Beetle

8. Soldier Beetle

6. Jansen Beetle

9. *Plastazote Corixa*

10. *Corixa*

11. Yellow *Corixa*

12. Floating Snail

13. *Dytiscus* Larva

14. Spider

9. Plaztazote Corixa

Hook length: 10mm
Thread: Brown
Abdomen: A piece of plastazote shaped, glued and slotted onto hook shank
Back and Oars: Pheasant tail fibres tied over back with two left extending to form oars

10. Corixa

Hook length: 10mm
Thread: Brown
Tag: Silver tinsel
Abdomen: Covered with lead wire or foil and dubbed with pale yellow angora wool
Rib: Silver wire
Back: Orange-brown raffia pulled tight
Hackle: Two bunches of brown hen fibres tied either side of body

11. Yellow Corixa

Hook length: 10mm
Thread: Brown
Abdomen: Primrose silk
Rib: Brown thread
Back: Olive-green goose fibres varnished
Oars: Two olive-green goose fibres

12. Floating Snail

Hook length: 8–10mm
Thread: Black or brown
Abdomen: Black or brown chenille in a ball shape

13. Dytiscus Larva

Hook length: 15–20mm
Thread: Black or brown
Tail: Short brown hackle fibres
Abdomen: Dirty yellow dubbing wick
Rib: Nylon tying thread
Thorax: As abdomen
Legs: Brown partridge hackle tied over thorax
Wing Case and Back: Brown p.v.c. Body Flex
Head: Brown marabou or brown dubbing
Eyes: Black bead chain

14. Spider

Hook length: 10mm
Thread: Brown
Abdomen: Brown seal's fur tied fat
Rib: Silver tinsel with tip at rear
Hackle: Brown Partridge

Miscellaneous 3

Hawthorn Fly (*Bibio Marci*)

This is a large black fly with a hairy body and very long hindlegs that trail well beyond the body in flight. The fly is on the wing for a very short time in late April, early May. In windy weather large numbers are often blown onto the water and greedily taken by the trout.

Bluebottle

A terrestrial fly that may very occassionally find its way onto the water. A stout fly with a blue-green metallic body and brown thorax.

Gravel Bed (*Hexatoma Fuscipennis*)

Small crane fly-shaped fly with pale brown wings with heavy veins. In the pupal stage it lives in the sand or gravel near the edge of rivers. They swarm near rivers in April, May and June and are often blown onto the water in large numbers.

Black Gnat (Various *Diptera* (*Bibio Johannis*))

The name, Black Gnat, covers several flies of the *Diptera* but they are so similar for fishing purposes that they are linked together. Swarms of Black Gnats are often seen over the water and are particularly vulnerable in windy weather. They are found at any time during the fishing season.

Crane Fly (*Tipulidae* (Daddy-Long-Legs))

A fly often blown onto the water on warm, windy days. There are nearly 300 species found from June to September.

Heather Fly (*Bibio Pomonae*)

The Heather Fly is related to the Hawthorn Fly, the main difference being the colour of its legs – the thigh part is a very bright red. It is more common in Scotland and only localized in parts of Wales and Northern England. Mostly found in late summer and early autumn.

Cow-Dung Fly (*Scatophaga Stercoraria*)

This is a yellow, hairy fly found in numbers on cow-pats near the river's edge. When blown onto the water trout will take them. A pattern is worth trying when cows are in the fields adjoining the river (see Miscellaneous 3 illustration).

1. Hawthorn

DRESSING

Hook length: 9–10mm
Thread: Black
Abdomen: Pheasant tail dyed black
Thorax: As abdomen
Legs: Pheasant tail dyed black and knotted
Wing: Traun River stonefly wing
Hackle: Black cock.
(See also Heather Fly, Miscellaneous 3 illustration)

2. Bluebottle

DRESSING

Hook length: 8–10mm
Thread: Black
Abdomen: Blue-green lurex
Rib: Black Ostrich herl
Wing: Blue-dun hackle tips tied flat over body
Hackle: Black cock

3. Gravel Bed (Clyde Sandfly)

DRESSING

Hook length: 10–12mm
Thread: Black
Abdomen: Black thread
Wing: Hen pheasant tail tied flat across the back
Hackle: Black cock

4. Gravel Bed

DRESSING

Hook length: 10–12mm
Thread: Dark Grey
Abdomen: Dark grey thread
Thorax: Mole's Fur
Hackle: Brown cock tied parachute

5. Black Gnat

DRESSING

Hook length: 5-8mm
Thread: Black
Abdomen: Black thread
Wing: Grey poly yarn tied flat
Hackle: Black cock

6. Black Gnat

DRESSING

Hook length: 5-8mm
Thread: Black
Abdomen: Dubbed black fur
Wing: Grey starling tied upright
Hackle: Black cock

7. Crane Fly (Daddy-Long-Legs)

DRESSING

Hook length: 20–30mm
Thread: Brown
Abdomen: Brown floss
Legs: Grey mono knotted
Wings: Ginger hackle points tied spent
Hackle: Ginger cock

8. Cranefly

DRESSING

Hook length: 20–30mm
Thread: Brown
Abdomen: Cinnamon turkey fibres
Legs: Cock pheasant tail fibres knotted to trail
Wings: Two badger cock tips tied over the body
Hackle: Ginger cock

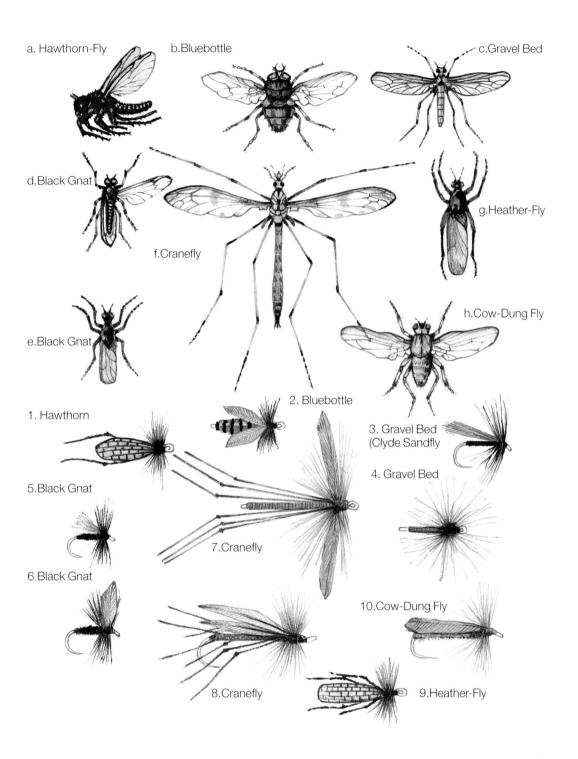

a. Hawthorn-Fly
b.Bluebottle
c.Gravel Bed
d.Black Gnat
f.Cranefly
g.Heather-Fly
e.Black Gnat
h.Cow-Dung Fly

1. Hawthorn
2. Bluebottle
3. Gravel Bed (Clyde Sandfly
4. Gravel Bed
5.Black Gnat
6.Black Gnat
7.Cranefly
8.Cranefly
9.Heather-Fly
10.Cow-Dung Fly

13 A Guide to Insect Identification

*Metamorphosis (*Plate A*)*

Before we become involved with the different aspects dealt with in this section of the book, I would just like to point out an act of nature that has a great bearing on the way we should design and use the artificial. This is the act of metamorphosis which brings about a change of shape and character in the 'flies' we use. I have illustrated some of these changes and stages of change in Plate A, and although all the main groups of insects we deal with go through some form of metamorphosis they do not all follow the same changes. Because this act of nature takes place and because the fish react to these changes, it follows that the successful flyfisher must, to some extent, be aware of and take into account these stages in the insect's life cycle, and to fish not only with the correct artificial but to fish it at the correct depth and in the correct manner to imitate the natural. The differences in the life cycles of all the main orders of flies are illustrated and explained under the relevant headings. Each section shows the natural going through its particular life cycle with relevant artificials to match these phases. The artificials shown are an example and, as you will observe from Section I of this book, there are a variety of choices available, so the artificial example shown should not be taken as the 'perfect' or only match.

Ephemeroptera

The egg stage is the point at which all the insect life cycles begin and although it has only a passing interest for the fly fisherman it is worthy of a mention. In the *Ephemeroptera*, most eggs are deposited by the female directly into the surface of the water. The eggs then sink and become randomly mixed in with the sand, stones, vegetation,and so forth, on, or near to the river or lake bed. There are some exceptions to this rule, some of the *baetis*, for instance, land on waterside vegetation, stones and so on, and crawl down these to deposit their eggs. At one time it was thought that all egg development took a long time but now it is known that there is a great deal of variation, some species develop over a matter of a few days and some over many months. Water temperatures and times of year also have a bearing on the hatching of the eggs.

We now come to the first stage of development that has a direct bearing on how we fish and the different artificials we use. Although all the upwinged flies have a nymphal stage, all nymphs do not behave in the same manner. After the eggs hatch the tiny nymphs emerge and develop by mostly feeding on decayed vegetable matter and algae. The nymph grows by moulting its larval skin, many moults taking place over a period of several months to two years.

Each of the different species of nymphs of the upwinged flies follow this pattern. We shall now consider how they differ.

Bottom Dwelling Nymphs of the *Ephemeroptera* (Plate B)

Ephemera (danica, vulgata):
These nymphs are silt burrowers and most of their lives are spent in tunnels on the river or lake bed. The *Ephemera* are the only nymphs in fact that actually do burrow to form tunnels. As can be seen from Plate B, the head is pointed and has strong mandibles capable of excavating silt on the river bed. They have

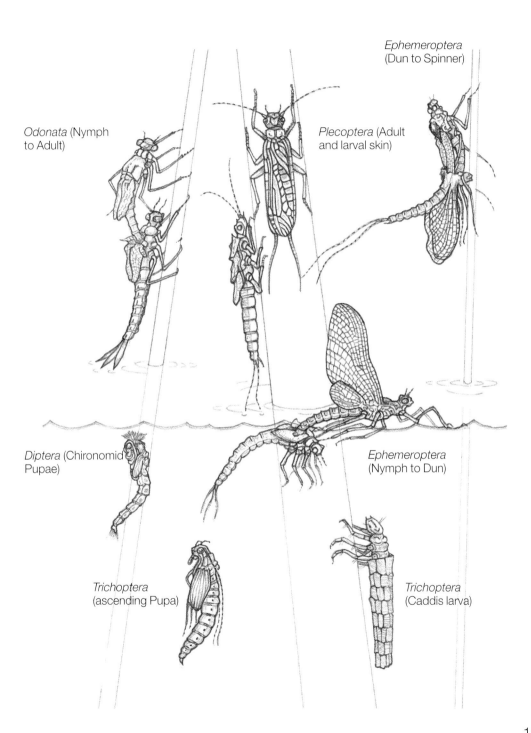

Ephemeroptera
(Dun to Spinner)

Odonata (Nymph
to Adult)

Plecoptera (Adult
and larval skin)

Diptera (Chironomid
Pupae)

Ephemeroptera
(Nymph to Dun)

Trichoptera
(ascending Pupa)

Trichoptera
(Caddis larva)

Plate B. *Ephemeroptera* bottom dwelling nymphs
(naturals and heavy weighted artificials)

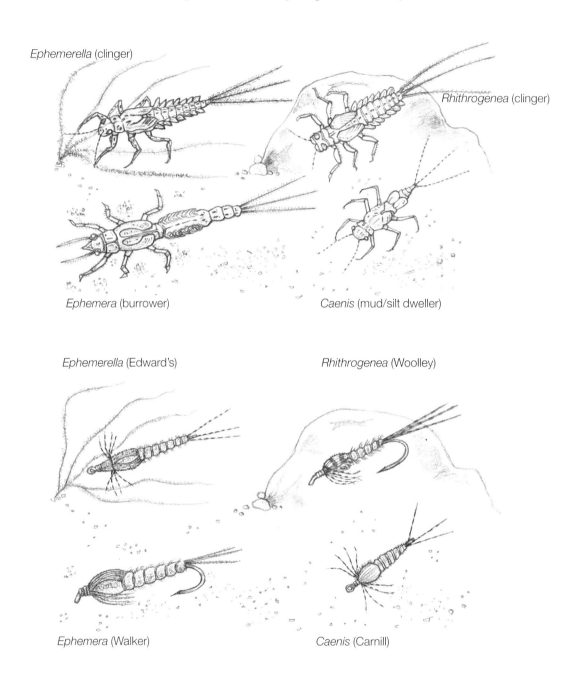

Ephemerella (clinger)

Rhithrogenea (clinger)

Ephemera (burrower)

Caenis (mud/silt dweller)

Ephemerella (Edward's)

Rhithrogenea (Woolley)

Ephemera (Walker)

Caenis (Carnill)

specially fine filaments running along each side of the abdomen which allow a constant flow of oxygenating water, containing food particles, to pass along the body. Because of its lifestyle the only time the mayfly nymph becomes available to the trout is around the time of the main mayfly hatch (Mayfly Fortnight). At this time the nymph starts to become active 'above ground' and so enters the trout's domain. Over the main mayfly time, say a week or two before experience tells us to expect it, during the hatch and a week or so after the hatch, a heavily weighted artificial fished along the bottom will account for feeding fish especially if there are few surface-hatching fly about.

Caenis:

The *caenis* is the upwinged fly also knows as the Broadwings or 'angler's curse', this last name being partly given to it because of the tiny size of the adult. The nymph is of such a size as to be almost impossible to copy and this, coupled with the fact that it spends its life on the river or lake bed amongst the silt, makes it almost of no importance to the fisherman in its nymphal stage. They spend their lives slowly crawling about amongst silt and debris searching out food. The size of hook required to match the size of the natural would be so small that it would not allow for the additional weight necessary to carry it to the river or lake bed.

Ephemerella:

The *Ephemerella* nymph can be found clinging or crawling very slowly amongst the stones and vegetation of river beds, particularly at the tail of reasonably fast-flowing stretches. The Blue Winged Olive is amongst this group of flies and is one of our most common and important species. The nymph should be heavily weighted whilst retaining a reasonably slim shape and fished dead drift just off the bottom.

Rhithrogena, Ecdyonurus, Heptagenia:

These are the stone-clinging nymphs. The nymphs in this group are sturdily built to cope with the environment in which they are found. They mostly inhabit the fast, turbulent water where they spend much of their time clinging to the stones and rocks. Although favouring the underside of stones, where they feed on the algae, their bodies are designed to withstand the pressure put upon them by flowing water. The body has a markedly flattened appearance and this, together with the flow of water over them, keeps the nymph pressed down upon the stones. Because of the head and body shape the nymph always faces upstream whatever movement it makes. The artificial nymph should take into account the overall structure of the natural – the head and wingcases are broad, the overall body shape is 'chunky'. This easily facilitates the additional weight necessary to fish the nymph dead drift off the bottom. When the additional weight is added to the hook in whatever form chosen, and before the dressing is added, the whole body shape should be flattened with small nosed pliers.

Mid-water dwelling nymphs of the *Ephemeroptera, Leptophlebia, Habrophlebia, Paraleptophlebia, Siphlonurus* (Plate C)

This group of nymphs are known as the laboured swimmers. They are of a medium-sized build and, as the group name suggests, they are not the most active of nymphs, although more prone to movement than the bottom-dwellers. Their skills at swimming range from poor to reasonable. Some of this group have pronounced gills and this is accommodated for in some of the fly dressings. The artificial should carry weight and be fished dead drift or with a slight movement of sink and draw; it should never be fished with pronounced movements.

Cloeon, Baetis, Centroptilum, Procloeon:

This group of nymphs contains some of the most important and best known of the

117

angler's flies, especially amongst the Baetis. Members of this group, for obvious reasons, are known as the Agile Darters and if disturbed or wishing to move can do so with a fair turn of speed. Their shape matches their accomplishments at swimming, they are strong but slim in appearance. They have long tails fringed with very fine hairs that help propel their streamlined bodies in and out of the weed growth that is their preferred habitat. Because they are the most active group of nymphs they can be found in all levels of water but prefer the mid-water range. Where there is a lot of weed growth large numbers of nymphs can be found. The artificial should be medium to lightly weighted and a little more movement can be given to these than in the previous groups. Small short bursts of speed can be imparted to the artificial for even this most active of the *Ephemeroptera* nymph groups never travels in yard-long dashes.

Surface and Sub-Surface Stages of the *Ephemeroptera* (Plate D)

When the nymph has reached maturity the next stage in the life cycle of the upwinged fly takes place. The mature nymph is ready to turn into the dun (sub-imago), the first stage of the winged adult. What triggers the nymph to rise to the surface in numbers at any one time is not fully understood but we have all experienced a fairly uneventful start to the day with few fish rising. At first a trickle of hatching fly appear, then a flotilla and with it the ensuing onslaught by hungry trout. There is no pattern to the event, some flies come off the water on hot, dry days, some seem to prefer damp wet conditions, others don't even mind the cold.

Before we get to the fully winged dun (the emerging stage), the half-way point between nymph and dun, is of great importance to the angler. At this point where the nymph pushes its back through the surface film to allow the dun to hatch out, it is in one of its most vulnerable positions. The time between the

nymph's case splitting and the dun pulling its wings and body clear of its former skin gives the trout ample time to intercept it. Even after emerging from the nymph's case the dun must rest for a short time to allow its wings to dry fully. The drying speed of the wings is, in part, dependent upon the weather conditions. If the air is cold, wet and damp the dun will take longer to get airborne than on hot, sunny days when it can leave the water very quickly.

The emerger artificial is a compromise stage; the hook bend and part of the shank are dressed to match the back half of the nymph and designed to trail under the water surface. The front half of the hook shank to the eye is designed to be the first stage of the dun pulling itself free of the nymph's case. The front half of the artificial has to sit, if possible, in a slightly backward sloping profile on the water surface. This sounds difficult but there are a range of flies designed to do just that and all of them work well. It follows from the above that the last segments of the nymph half of the fly may require a little added weight, perhaps in the form of wire and the front emerging dun part should contain some buoyant material, the addition of drooping tails and straggly legs helping to complete the design. The emerger pattern is a very useful fly to fish because, to some extent, it removes the guesswork on what stage the fish are feeding. If the fish are taking rising nymphs just under the surface, the rear half of the patterns tied to represent the nymph's case will attract the fish's attention. If the fish are feeding on the dun then the whole image of the artificial resting on the surface will be sufficient to take fish. The emerger is best of all fished dead drift avoiding any form of drag. During the first part of the hatch fish may stay for a long time feeding on emergers before turning their attention to the fully formed dun.

The next stage we consider is the fully formed dun. Having parted with the nymphal case the dun will float on the water surface for a while, all the time at the mercy of the wind and water flow. If, at this point, the natural's movements are observed by a feeding trout

Plate C. *Ephemeroptera* mid-water dwelling nymphs (naturals and medium to light weighted artificials)

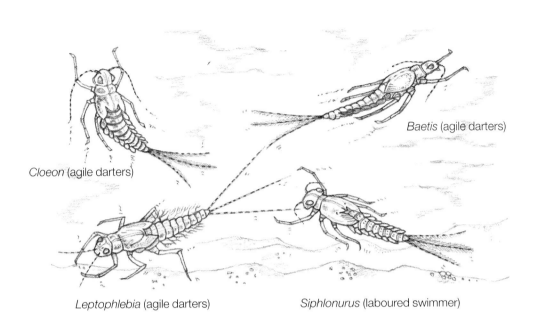

Cloeon (agile darters)

Baetis (agile darters)

Leptophlebia (agile darters)

Siphlonurus (laboured swimmer)

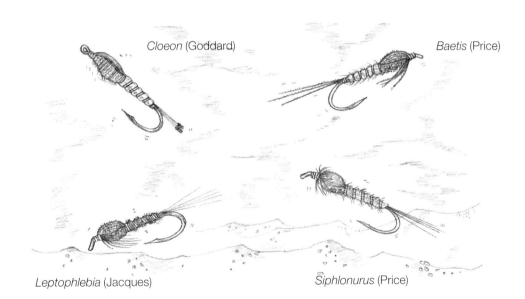

Cloeon (Goddard)

Baetis (Price)

Leptophlebia (Jacques)

Siphlonurus (Price)

Plate D. *Ephemeroptera* surface and sub-surface stages
(naturals and floating or non-weighted artificials)

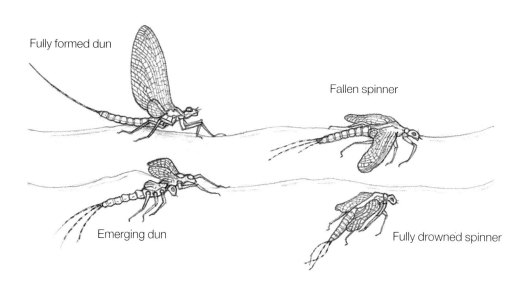

Fully formed dun

Fallen spinner

Emerging dun

Fully drowned spinner

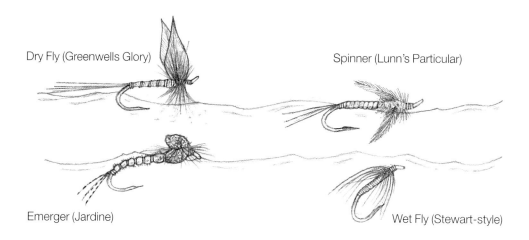

Dry Fly (Greenwells Glory)

Spinner (Lunn's Particular)

Emerger (Jardine)

Wet Fly (Stewart-style)

the fly will meet a speedy end. If sufficient flies are hatching out and being conveyed by the stream one after the other over the trout's stations, most fish will go into a fairly regular feeding pattern. On seeing this, we would now turn to fishing the dry fly, matching it as accurately as possible to the natural. The patterns of dry flies are endless, especially to match the *Ephemeroptera*, and some of the styles and choices become purely personal, mostly through trial and error until you end up with a selection that gives you confidence in their effectiveness. The tying of the dry fly can go from a fairly simple basic design – dubbed body, wound cock hackle – to the more elaborate designs of Goddard and Clarke's USD Paraduns. Although the body design of the dry fly is a fairly basic shape, many styles have appeared to represent the wing shapes and the legs. The basic wing/legs representation is a cock hackle wound in at the eye end of the hook, the upward fibres to represent the wing, the downward fibres to represent the legs. A fairly sparse tying would probably suggest the fly at rest. A more elaborate use of the hackle would represent wing movement. Some patterns have the hackle at the reverse end of the hook, which holds the barbed end out of the water and stops it being visible to the trout. To the addition of the basic vertically wound cock hackle we sometimes have wings in the form of starling, moorhen, cut wings or poly yarn type wings. Some flies have loop wings made from feather or man-made fibres. The hackle itself can, instead of being tied in the vertical style, be wound in horizontally parachute style. The hackle is usually wound round a wing or post of poly yarn. In the more elaborate style of the parachute tying, the whole fly is tied upside down so that the bend of the hook is above the water. This probably gives the most accurate imitation of the dun yet devised.

Another variation on the vertical hackle is the funnelduns, devised by Neil Patterson. The hackle in this case is tied further back along the shank and pulled forward 'funnelled' round the eye of the hook at about 45 degrees. Some styles do not use any form of hackle, for example, the Richards and Swishers series of No-hackle Duns utilize the buoyant materials to form the body and thus keep the fly floating. They rely on the wings being the main triggers to rise the trout. The drawback to this theory is that you can fish floating patterns without wings, say parachute style. The argument then would be that the wings aren't the main triggers to the trout but light patterns created by the feet. Everything in fly fishing is a contradiction yet, I repeat what I have said before – it is the overall impressions of the naturals we seek and these, in the case of the dry fly, should be tails, body, wings and legs. If you can match the artificial fairly closely to the drifting duns you will take fish during the hatch periods. Most duns floating down do not make any movements, their journey downstream is by the power of water flow and wind. It follows that the artificial should do the same. Once a feeding fish is observed the dry fly should be cast a reasonable distance above him, allowance being made to avoid any drag. If there is a lot of surface activity, fly presentation must be accurate; the trout will not feel it necessary to move his position to intercept passing flies since there will be enough passing directly overhead. In sparse hatches the fish will be more inclined to travel a short way to take its food. In all *Ephemeroptera* dry fly fishing conditions, upstream, across stream or even downstream, the same rules apply. *Ephemeroptera* duns do not cause much, if any, surface disturbance.

We will now move on to the next stage of development in the natural, sub-imago to imago, dun to spinner. The spinner stage in the lifecycle of the fly is arrived at after another wonder in the life of these incredible creatures. Imagine having three layers of cling film, the two outer layers dull, the inner layer bright and shiny. You have to pull the inner layer out without a mark or crease and you aren't allowed to touch the outer layers in any way. Sounds impossible, yet there is a creature that can accomplish this task in one smooth movement, not only removing new wings from inside old wings but new legs from old legs and new body from old body. We now arrive at a beauty and perfection to be wondered at – the imago or spinner. Even the colours of the fly have undergone a transformation. This final stage of its life may only last a few hours. The imago usually collect in swarms over or away from the water and mating takes place.

Different species swarm in different areas, some preferring to mate over the water, others over the shore area and others well away from the water itself. Swarming mostly takes place during daylight and once a male locates a female, mating takes place almost immediately and nearly always in flight. The copulation period is very short and the flies soon separate. The female now flies back over the water to start egg laying. The only male spinners that end up on the water in any number are the species that mate over the water. The female spinner, having returned to the water surface, begins to deposit her eggs. Most species lay their eggs directly into the water whilst flying upstream. Others land or go under water to release their eggs. With this final act accomplished the female spinner falls to the surface and dies and once again provides food for the watchful trout. The position of the spent fly on the water has now to be considered for the design of the artificial. The body, tails and legs trail backwards, the wings are outstretched sloping slightly to the rear. The body of the artificial is tied along the hook in the normal way. Tails are usually splayed out and made of feather fibres or man-made fibres and are fairly stiff. The spent wing can be hackle fibres, hackle tips, poly yarn and even clear polythene cut to shape. If legs are represented it is usually done with a sparse hackle or the thorax picked out to avoid the fly sitting out of the water. The artificial must be designed to lie on or in the surface film. In other words, the hook shank wants to be flush with the water surface. Because the natural is in this position it can be easily overlooked by the fisherman but not the fish.

If fish are taking off the surface and you can see no sign of emerging duns it is worth trying a spinner pattern especially in the evening or first thing in the morning. It is always worthwhile looking in still water or calm areas near the bank to see if any spinners are present. This tactic holds true for most food forms available at any time to the trout. Because the spent female is at, or near, death she naturally makes little movement, perhaps just a little twitching that sends concentric circles fading from her on the water surface. These disturbances are so minor that it is not possible or necessary to imitate them when fishing the artificial. The artificial should be left to float naturally on the water surface.

The last act of the *Ephemeroptera* is to end up as a meal for one of the river's occupants or to be swept away by the river's flow. The fully drowned spinner tumbling along through the water can be imitated by a sparsely tied wet fly such as a stewart-style spider pattern.

Plecoptera

The *Plecoptera* or Stoneflies lay their eggs directly onto the water surface. The eggs sink to the bottom where they become attached to the rocks and stones. Hatching times vary from several days to many weeks and water temperatures and so forth must have some bearing on the length of time taken.

The Nymph (Plate E)

The first stage of development of real interest to the fly fisherman is that of the nymph. Although there is a large variation in the size of the various species of nymphs they are all strong and reasonably active creatures. The nymphs are different from the *Ephemeroptera* nymphs in that they have only two tails and the head antennae are longer. The size of the species seems to have some bearing on the length of time the nymph takes to reach maturity. The smaller species take from one to one-and-a-half years and the larger up to three years. Stoneflies generally prefer faster

Plate E. *Plectoptera* surface and sub-surface stages
(Naturals weighted nymphs and floating adults)

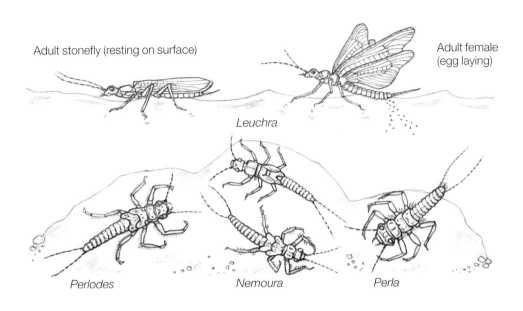

Adult stonefly (resting on surface)

Adult female (egg laying)

Leuchra

Perlodes

Nemoura

Perla

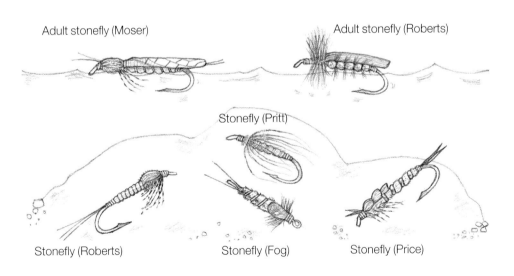

Adult stonefly (Moser)

Adult stonefly (Roberts)

Stonefly (Pritt)

Stonefly (Roberts)

Stonefly (Fog)

Stonefly (Price)

running water than most mayflies but there are some variations in both species. Food also varies between the species of stonefly; larger species prefer aquatic larvae and so on, but will also eat vegetable matter, while the smaller nymphs are herbivorous. Stoneflies, as their name suggests, prefer stony lakes and rivers. The nymphs are known as bottom-crawlers or 'creepers' and, although they can swim, they seldom do. As they grow, some nymphs will moult up to thirty times before reaching maturity. Before the final moult the enlarged wing pads will start to blacken. The stonefly nymph lives a similar lifestyle to the stone-clinging nymphs of the *Ephemeroptera* and so some of the nymph designs of the artificials are also similar. The great difference between the *Ephemeroptera* artificial nymphs and those of the stoneflies is the fact most *Ephemeroptera* species have tyings specific to the particular species, the stonefly patterns tend to be more of a general design. This fact can be partly accounted for in the distribution of stoneflies, some rivers have good populations whilst in others the numbers are erratic, and in lowland weedy waters only a few species are found. This, coupled with the fact that hatches of *Ephemeroptera* and *Trichoptera* are more stable and significant on most rivers, has somewhat, in fly fishing terms, put the stoneflies into a second-class citizen role. For all this there are a good number of nymph patterns available. Because of the stonefly's preference for stony-bottomed faster flowing rivers, the artificial must be well weighted and fished along the bottom. They are not particularly speedy movers so only a slight movement needs to be imparted to the artificial otherwise let it fish with the flow. One of the main differences between these and the *Ephemeroptera* nymphs are the accentuated wing pads and these should be emphasized in the dressing.

The next stage in the lifecycle of the *Plecoptera*, although of no interest in fishing terms, is worthy of a mention. The nymph of the stonefly, unlike that of the *Ephemeroptera*, does not hatch out in full view of the trout. The mature nymph crawls onto a stone or some form of vegetation, or even the shore or bank area of the river, the final nymph's skin splits across the wing pad area and the winged adult emerges. Many of the male flies have very short wings and they are incapable of flight. Although females have larger wings and are capable of flight they prefer to move about on the ground rather than fly. Adult stoneflies live only for a few days and are always found near water. Very soon after emergence of the females, which usually occurs a few days after the males, mating takes place on the ground. Adult stoneflies only live for a few days so the female has to return to the water fairly quickly to release her eggs. This brings us to the next stage of the life of the *Plecoptera* to interest the fisherman.

Adult and Egg-laying Stonefly (Plate E)

At times adult stoneflies will arrive by one means or another onto the water surface, even if not in the process of egg laying. This is called the resting position and it can be clearly seen from the illustration that the overall shape of the adult is quite distinct from the *Ephemeroptera* adult. The body will be flat across the water surface and the wings, which are hard and shiny, will be held fairly flat running along the length of the body. Those with tails have two and these are fairly short. In some of the smaller species the wings have a rolled appearance when at rest. Some of the earlier patterns were tied more in the shape of the *Ephemeroptera*, a vertical hackle, sloping back wings and long tails. More accurate patterns are available and the hackle, more suitable for other duties than a stonefly, has given way to feather slip wings and man-made wings. In the case of feather slip wings the two feathers, preferably stiff in fibre, should be cut to shape and tied in over a more substantial body than the upwinged fly body. The man-made wings can be produced from material such as synthetic curtains, coloured and cut to shape. 'Off the shelf' wings are available, these are preformed and very lifelike, as is the case with Roman Moser's wings. The narrower needle flies and so on, cannot be copied in this way but a method of winging needle flies has been produced by Chauncy Lively, an American. One hackle is used and this is shaped by pulling the hackle fibres back on themselves along the stalk and varnishing to produce a stiff feather that is tied in flat to the body. The actual fly is illustrated in Chapter 7 of this book under Wonderwing Stonefly. The returning female flying over the water and depositing her eggs onto the surface requires a little more 'buzz' about the tying. The flat wing can be retained or given a slightly more upward sloping profile from front to rear. Now introduce a short fibred cock hackle to the front of the wing – this helps on the underside to act as legs and also carry the body in a sloping rearwards shape. The top hackles along with the more solid wing, give the appearance of movement that you would see in the adult. The resting stonefly should be fished fairly static perhaps with an occasional twitch to the fly. The egg-laying adult can be fished in a series of little jig movements with very short rests in between, somewhat similar to fishing the adult sedge that we shall describe under *Trichoptera*.

Trichoptera

The *Trichoptera* or Caddis or Sedge Flies starting with the egg. The female Caddis fly lays her eggs directly onto the water surface, into the water on waterside plants and on stones. Eggs are mostly laid in one mass or in strings although species in the free-swimming group lay eggs in smaller groups and some singly. Hatching is over a reasonably short period, anything up to three weeks. After this time very small soft-bodied nymphs appear. In the species where eggs were laid on the bankside the nymphs quickly make their way into the water. Most caddis species begin to build protective cases around their bodies but there are a few exceptions – the free-living or free-swimming forms. As the caddis larva begins to develop, the case in which it lives

has to be continually enlarged. This is done by adding material to the front end of the case, the material being held in place by a sticky, silk thread produced by the larva. The shapes and materials used for the case are many and varied.

Although it is possible to identify certain species by the materials and shape of the case produced this is not true in all sedge flies. The case itself is hollow to facilitate movement and allow a constant flow of oxygenating water over the larva. Some cases are partly designed to suit the conditions under which a particular species lives but also to take into account material available. For instance in fast-flowing water, pebbles and stones are available. These, built into the case, help to prevent the caddis being swept downstream. The front opening of the case is large enough for the larva's head and legs to protrude to enable movement. Most cased caddis are omnivorous – the net spinners will take any form of food and the free-swimming forms being more agile prefer a diet of micro animal life.

Bottom-dwelling Caddis Larvae (Plate F)

Under nearly every stone and amongst every clump of weeds in the river the angler will find caddis. Because the cased caddis is a bottom dweller, especially the species found in faster flows, the artificial must be well weighted and drifted along the riverbed. The basic design is similar in all the cased artificials, the hook shank being either dubbed or built up of any artificial materials to match the naturals. In some of the more 'realistic' designs the actual materials used by the naturals are incorporated into the artificial; for instance, following an underbody of lead wire or similar, an overbody of floss is wound and then covered in glue and rolled in fine sand. In front of the case is usually wound a short fibred hackle and in front of this some form of head. The short fibred hackle represents the protruding legs. Because of the nature of cased caddis with all the extra weight they carry, movement is very slow and laboured. The artificial must be fished in a similar manner – dead drift, or with the slightest of movement. In stillwater conditions slightly more movement can be imparted to the artificial.

Free-swimming Larvae (Plate F)

The non-case-making larvae have tougher bodies than the case-makers for obvious reasons. Their body shape and segmentation is similar to that of the common garden caterpillar. Although they are sometimes called free-swimming they prefer to crawl about on the rocks and vegetation of the river or lake bed. The artificial is a reasonably easy tying and is usually made up of a dubbed body with a back of p.v.c., raffene, latex, and so forth, stretched along the full length of the body. The segmentation of the natural is usually emphasized by the use of some form of ribbing, wire, mono nylon, tying thread, and so on. Legs are created with a very sparse short hackle, partridge or similar, or a short beard hackle. Alternatively, the thorax dubbing is picked out. To this is added some form of head either dubbed or formed with the tying thread. The artificial is reasonably weighted and fished slowly with an occasional twitch so that it slightly rises from the bottom. The natural larva reaching maturity now goes into the next stage of development and begins to pupate.

Pupa and Emerger Stage (Plate G)

In order to pupate, the cased caddis and the free-living caddis attach themselves to submerged objects, stones, and so on, by means of a secreted substance from the larva. Non-case making larva now make some form of chamber in which they spin a cocoon. All forms now prepare to pupate. After several days or up to a few weeks, the fully formed pupa bites through the silken cocoon with the aid of its powerful jaws, and using its strong legs makes its way to the water surface. Some species emerge on the water surface whilst others will climb up plant stems to hatch out into the fully winged adult. The pupal stage has fascinated the fly tier and many and varied are the patterns available, some of which are excellent, see Plate G. Some pupae artificials are weighted, others are tied to fish just sub-surface. The weighted patterns should be fished sink and draw to match the natural making its way to the surface. Sub-surface patterns should be allowed to drift naturally. The artificial pattern, weighted or not, has a segmented body; this is either some form of dubbing, latex, nylon mono, and so on. The main aim is to form a taper from the thorax to the hook bend with prominent segmentation, the tying thread or wire forming the ribbing of the body. The other main features in the natural to be copied are the wingcases and the trailing antennae and legs. This is achieved with the use of raffene, feather slips, and so forth. Legs and antennae are created by the use of partridge hackle, pheasant tail, herl or similar. The emerger stage is very similar to the pupal stage but more of the artificial needs to protrude above the water surface. To achieve this buoyancy, materials are tied in at the top end of the fly, deer hair in a muddler style or some other buoyant material picked out to form a straggly shape. Add to this some soft hackle fibres to match the emerging legs and we have a reasonable impression of the natural. The artificial should be fished in the surface film either naturally or with some slight twitching movement. Once the adult breaks free of the pupa we arrive at the fully winged sedge.

Resting and Egg-laying Sedge (Plate G)

When the adult sedge has emerged from the pupa it takes a short rest period during which the wings harden. At this point the ungainly sedge makes every attempt to take to the air. It takes some time before the newly hatched sedge becomes a competent flier, and in its first efforts to get off the water surface it can attract some rapid response from the

Plate F. *Trichoptera* bottom dwelling and free-swimming larva (natural and weighted and semi-weighted artificials)

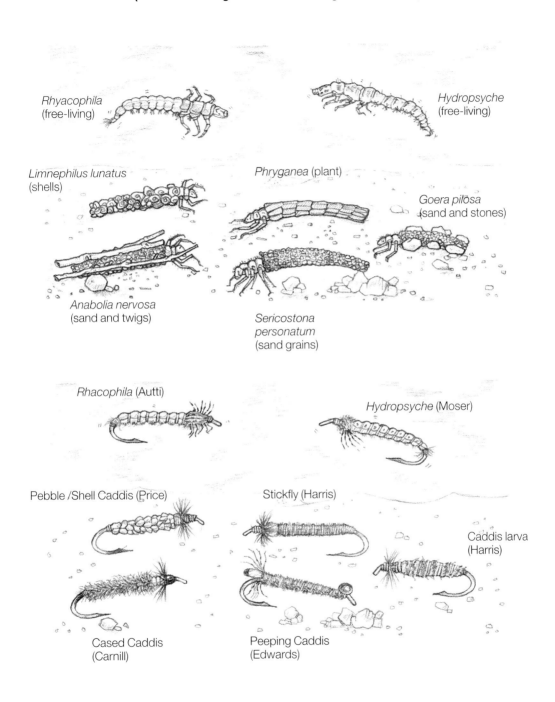

Rhyacophila
(free-living)

Hydropsyche
(free-living)

Limnephilus lunatus
(shells)

Phryganea (plant)

Goera pilosa
(sand and stones)

Anabolia nervosa
(sand and twigs)

Sericostona
personatum
(sand grains)

Rhacophila (Autti)

Hydropsyche (Moser)

Pebble /Shell Caddis (Price)

Stickfly (Harris)

Caddis larva
(Harris)

Cased Caddis
(Carnill)

Peeping Caddis
(Edwards)

Plate G. *Trichoptera* surface and sub-surface stages
(naturals and floating or non-weighted artificials)

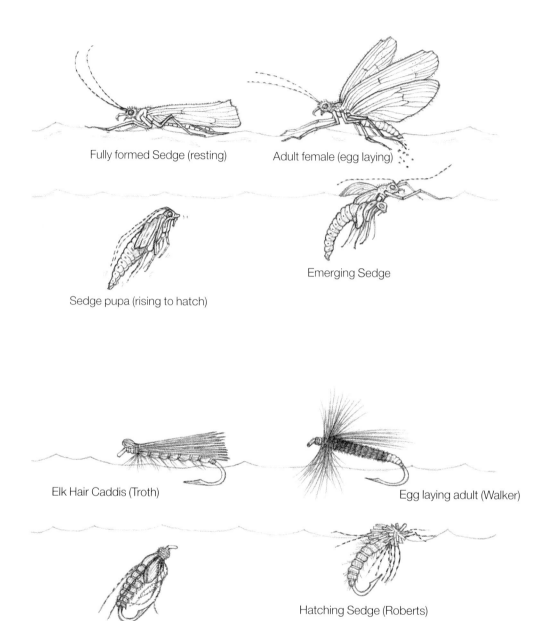

Fully formed Sedge (resting)

Adult female (egg laying)

Sedge pupa (rising to hatch)

Emerging Sedge

Elk Hair Caddis (Troth)

Egg laying adult (Walker)

Hatching Sedge pupa (Edwards)

Hatching Sedge (Roberts)

watchful trout. The resting sedge has roof-shaped wings and is more like the resting stonefly than the adult *Ephemeroptera*. In the resting position the body runs parallel to the water surface and very close to it, the legs are spread out and the wings overlap the body length.

Artificials in this position have a dubbed fur or synthetic body – the body can be picked out to represent legs or, alternatively, a short palmered cock can be used. The wings are tied over the body in a tent shape formed from feather slips, elk or deer hair, and even such things as polypropylene yarn can be used so long as the correct wing shape is achieved. Some designs will also include the forward protruding antennae which should be made from something stiff and durable.

We now come to the flying sedge leaving or returning to the water to lay her eggs. After the sedge has escaped from the water surface it can, depending on the species, be seen in small swarms over the water. Most of the sedges mate whilst at rest and after mating the female returns to lay her eggs. It is only the ones that lay directly onto the water surface that become obvious to trout. Whether taking off or returning to the water, the sedge causes a lot of erratic movement and trout will take them in a like manner.

Because of this variety of movement, exaggerated images must be apparent to the trout and a lot of artificials take this into consideration, being somewhat overstated in their dressings. This is one fly that should be fished on the surface with movement – even a dragging artificial that in the upwinged patterns would put a feeding fish down, when dragged across a sedge taking trout will excite it to rise.

Because of this, most artificials are tied to look fairly bushy with palmered bodies, generous hackles, shaped wings. The best phrase to sum up the dressings and the way the fly is fished is to say the artificial must not be demure but should be obvious on the water.

Diptera

The *Diptera* are a very large order of flies known as two-winged or true flies, or to the angler, the flat-winged flies. Only a few of this vast range of flies are of interest to the fisherman. The two most important are the Midges and Gnats. The female midge will fly low over the water depositing her eggs in enormous numbers that attach themselves to water plants or other objects in the water.

The tiny larvae that hatch out, swim down to the river or lake bed where they live in the mud or silt. The larvae can occur in a range of colours from transparent through to shades of yellow-brown, green and through to the best known of all, blood red 'bloodworms'.

The Red Larva and the Phantom Larva (Plate H)

As the name bloodworm suggests the larva is exactly like a small worm but with two very tiny false legs at the head and tail. During its life as a larva it will often leave the safety of the lower water levels to absorb oxygen from the better oxygenated areas of the water. It is during these trips that it leaves itself open to being preyed upon by trout.

Because of the simple form of the naturals the artificial is a very simple tying. The hook is basically covered in the relevant natural colour, in the case of the 'bloodworm' that colour is blood red. The body is made from feather fibres, floss silk, and so on and is usually lengthened by adding a 'tail' of feather fibres. Ribbing is done with thread, tinsel or lurex.

Phantom larva are dressed in a similar way with grey floss or very pale silk. The artificial is fished in a twitching motion with short rests to let the larva sink a little in a natural manner. After many moults the tiny larva change into the pupal stage. They now leave the lake or river bed and make their way to the surface.

Midge and Phantom Pupa (Plate H)

This is another stage in the life cycle of a particular insect that has caught the imagination of the fly tier and some wonderful patterns have been designed. In shape, but not size, some of the artificials are similar to those of the sedge pupa. The pupa, like the larva, varies in size and colour, it has a bend to its body and is obviously segmented. It has a pronounced thorax area with wing buds and white breathing filaments to the head and white hairs to the tail area. The speed at which it rises to the surface varies and occasionally 'rest' periods are taken on the way up. On arriving at the surface some pupae will hang for a considerable time before the thorax splits and the adult emerges. The artificial is tied in a very similar way to the sedge pupa. The body is tied, curved and tapering from the thorax area and can be silk or wool, feather fibres, dubbing and so on. This is sometimes covered with polythene or p.v.c. The body should always be ribbed with wire or fine thread. At the rear of the body white fibres or floss are used for the tails; this is also added for the breathing filaments at the head. Added to this is a thorax area of herl, fur or, to aid floatation, spun deer hair. In the famous John Goddard pattern, an Ethafoam ball wrapped in ladies tights material is used. The pupa is usually fished near to the surface and either left completely still or in a slow, steady sink and draw action. After the pupa arrives at the surface the adult begins to break free and leaves the pupal shuck behind.

Emerger and Adult Stages (Plate H)

Adults and emergers can be present on nearly every day of the fishing season. Although once thought of as a 'stillwater' fly, more and more anglers are becoming aware of their importance on the rivers. Their growing presence is partly due to silting and pollution, the two things so disliked by the

other groups of flies do not pose the same problems for the *Diptera*. The emerger is basically of the same design as other designs of emergers. The rear half is still that of the pupa but now resting at a slight angle to the water surface with the legs of the adult fly reaching out forwards and the emerging wings, flat in this case, trailing towards the rear. The adult midge does not pose a complicated image on the surface – a thin body with fairly straggly legs and flat wings over the back. The artificial's body is tied from herl, dubbings, floss silk, ribbed in some patterns with hackle stalk, tying silk and so forth. Wings are usually kept white or very pale and flat over the body. Add to this a reasonably pronounced thorax of dubbing with a sparse hackle and the overall impression is complete. Some tyings dispense with obvious wings and rely on a slim body with a parachute wound hackle to act as legs and wings. Other adult patterns are designed to create a 'busier' effect or, in the case of very small species, to give the impression of two or more insects on the one hook. The knotted midge, John Veniard's tying, places a cock hackle at both ends of the hook covered with black floss. The *Diptera* should not be overlooked even by the river fisherman. Sometimes takes are very gentle, 'a dimple rise', and if no flies are apparent and you have gone through spinners and nymphs, a small pupa imitation is worth a try.

Odonata

The Dragonflies and Damselflies belong to the order *Odonata* and are amongst the largest and most easily recognized of British insects. Apart from their size, some are vividly coloured and the dragonflies can show amazing skill in flight. The damselflies are weaker fliers and do not have the ability to hover like the dragonflies. Although similar in shape the damselfly is slender in build and when at rest holds its wings together over its back. The larger dragonfly cannot fold its wings and they must always be open

Plate H. *Diptera* surface and sub-surface stages (naturals and floating, weighted and non-weighted artificials)

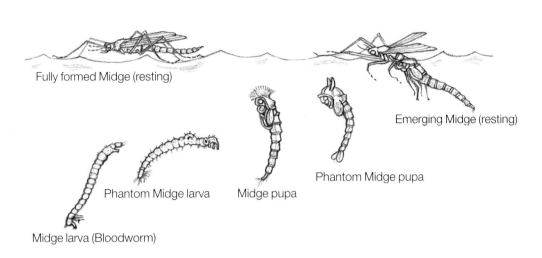

Fully formed Midge (resting)

Emerging Midge (resting)

Phantom Midge pupa

Phantom Midge larva

Midge pupa

Midge larva (Bloodworm)

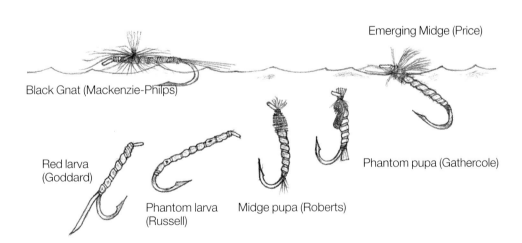

Emerging Midge (Price)

Black Gnat (Mackenzie-Philps)

Red larva (Goddard)

Phantom larva (Russell)

Midge pupa (Roberts)

Phantom pupa (Gathercole)

Plate I. *Odonata* Dragonflies and Damselflies surface and sub-surface stages (naturals,floating and weighted artificials)

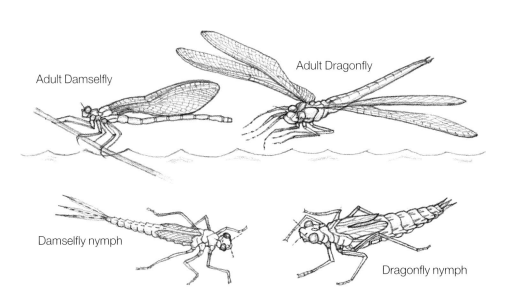

Adult Damselfly

Adult Dragonfly

Damselfly nymph

Dragonfly nymph

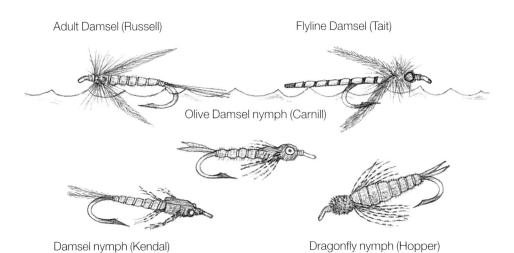

Adult Damsel (Russell)

Flyline Damsel (Tait)

Olive Damsel nymph (Carnill)

Damsel nymph (Kendal)

Dragonfly nymph (Hopper)

horizontally. The females of both species lay their eggs by reaching through the surface film or climbing down water plants and depositing the eggs fully submerged. With the tips of their abdomens they make an incision into the plant tissue and insert the eggs. Some of the species drop their eggs in masses or singly amongst weed beds or in areas of relative safety. Eggs laid in the latter part of the year may overwinter but others deposited earlier will take just a few weeks to hatch. The nymph may go through fifteen moults before becoming mature. This is usually over a twelve-month period in the damselfly but some dragonflies take up to five years.

Nymphs of the Dragonfly and the Damselfly (Plate I)

It is this stage of the lifecycle of these flies that is of particular interest to trout and therefore to trout fishermen. The basic difference between the two nymphs is that of size, the dragonfly being stouter and stronger than the damselfly. Both nymphs are voracious predators and few aquatic invertebrates are safe – worms, tadpoles and even small fish will be taken. The nymphs are usually found hunting slowly amongst vegetation and water plants. Both species can propel themselves through the water; the damselfly uses its body and undulates using its 'gills' as fins for swimming. The dragonfly nymph takes in water and, by means of pulsations of the abdomen wall, jets the water out of the rear of the abdomen causing the nymph to thrust forward. These movements have to be taken into consideration when fishing the nymph. Because most movement is slow and deliberate with short bursts of speed, especially in the damselfly, the artificial, well weighted, should be made to emulate these movements.

The design of the nymphs follows the natural. In the damselfly, the nymph is slim and usually brown-olive-green in colour with slim legs, wing buds and three leaf-like tails; the eyes are large and prominent. The artificial's body is usually of olive-brown

dubbing ribbed with fine wire; tails can be tied with olive hackle tips and the thorax is a fatter version of the body. Wingcases are added with feather fibres, legs can be made from partridge fibres or by the addition of a small cock hackle. Eyes are created from the melted ends of monofilament line. The dragonfly nymph can be created in the same manner but it must be remembered that they are altogether bulkier than the damselfly. When the natural nymph reaches maturity it climbs out of the water usually up bankside vegetation and sheds its larval skin (see Plate A). This stage is of no interest to the fly fisherman from a fishing point of view. When the adult has removed itself from the nymphal skin it takes some time, usually requiring warmth, before it can fly away.

Adult Damselfly and Dragonfly (Plate I)

Although the adult dragonfly is a joy to watch, it is of little interest to the fisherman. Some damselfly imitations are available because at times the slower, less active damselfly does fall prey to the trout. The artificial is tied with a slim body, usually extending beyond the length of the hook and most patterns are blue in colour. Wings are tied spent using cock hackle tips and legs are formed with a short, fibred cock hackle; in some patterns eyes are added. In the clever Dave Tait design, Ethafoam balls are used covered in mesh stocking. The artificial is usually fished dead drift, preferably amongst weed beds on hot sunny days when the natural is on the wing.

Miscellaneous

Shrimp, Water Louse, Alderfly, Hawthorn Fly (Plate J)

The shrimp and water louse are so similar in imitation and lifestyle that I shall put them together and concentrate on the shrimp, but what is said about one is roughly relevant to the

Plate J. Miscellaneous 1
surface and sub-surface stages
(naturals, floating and weighted artificials)

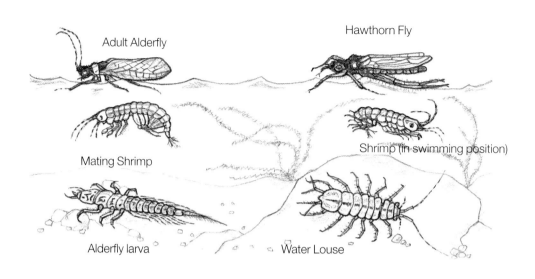

Adult Alderfly

Hawthorn Fly

Mating Shrimp

Shrimp (in swimming position)

Alderfly larva

Water Louse

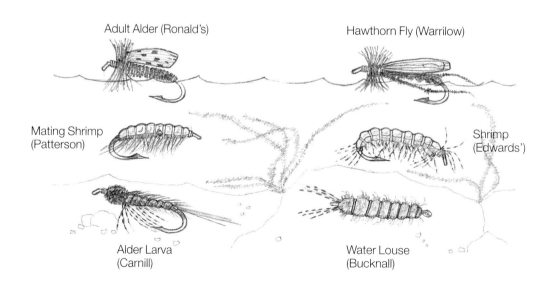

Adult Alder (Ronald's)

Hawthorn Fly (Warrilow)

Mating Shrimp
(Patterson)

Shrimp
(Edwards')

Alder Larva
(Carnill)

Water Louse
(Bucknall)

other. I have a great affection for the humble shrimp having caught hundreds of fish, particularly on the Oliver Edwards' pattern of it. It is, I think, quite obvious why, and most of it is not down to skill. Shrimp are always available to the trout in the rivers in which they thrive. The trout population must see them day in, day out and do not, as with other 'flies', have to get used to them before accepting them as a food item. There is no complicated life cycle with the shrimp. Eggs are carried around in a brood pouch between the female's legs and when fully developed they hatch into small replicas of the adult. Male shrimps are larger than females and both are translucent grey in colour. They have a curved body, slightly compressed from the sides and many limbs. Most movement is in a sideways direction and they swim in a peculiar jerky stop-start motion. When in mating colour they change from grey to orange-brown. At this time male and female travel around together and present a larger target than normal for the trout. The mating artificial is also acceptable in larger sizes than the grey 'form'. When fishing the artificial you can drift it down with the current or preferably add a little movement. If you can see the fish then lifting the artificial at the last moment will sometimes encourage a take. I remember once drifting a shrimp over a particular trout about ten times, either leaving it to come over him naturally or, at times, lifting the shrimp under his nose. He would not take it. The next cast the shrimp snagged in some short weed on a stone just to the side of the fish. He leisurely turned his head and sucked the artificial in. The copy of the shrimp is usually tied on a 'shrimp' hook which gives the curved appearance of the natural. Tying the body follows a similar pattern in most artificials, that is, some form of dubbing with longer strands in the form of hackle fibres and so on, left protruding to form legs. Backs are usually made from clear p.v.c. or polythene and ribbed with nylon mono or wire. The shrimp is tied in two basic colours, grey and orange-brown. Hooks are weighted, sometimes by adding lead strips to the top of the shank so turning the shrimp fish upside down.

Alderfly Larva and Adult (Plate J)

The female alderfly lays her eggs in batches on waterside vegetation. The larvae, after emerging, make their way to the mud and silt on the bottom where they live out this stage of their lives. They are voracious predators and will take caddis larvae, nymphs and any other invertebrate. After a period of up to two years in which the larva will have moulted up to nine times in order to put on growth, it leaves the bottom silt and makes its way to the water-side bank in order to pupate. After digging a small hole in which to secrete itself, pupation takes place and in about two weeks the adult fly emerges. Adult flies are not actually fond of flying and spend most of their time amongst the riverbank plants and stones. There are imitations of the winged fly but most fisher-men do not regard them to be of any particular importance, although some must be taken by trout when they inadvert-ently end up on the water. The larva is another matter for it will readily be taken by trout. The larva is long with a blunt head tapering down the body to a single tail. It has powerful jaws and long, slender, feathery gills down each side of the body. The artificial should be weighted and fished slowly along the bottom. Artificials are tied stressing the prominent points. The body is tied long and tapering from dubbed brown-ginger fur. The tail is tied from feather fibres, usually of a light colour or white marabou. A rib of gold tinsel or wire is run the length of the body. The thorax area is darker and tied from hare's ear fur or brown dubbing. Gills are made from palmering a ginger hen hackle the length of the body or running two strips of white marabou down each side. Legs are nearly always created out of brown partridge.

The Hawthorn Fly (Plate J)

The Hawthorn fly is only on the wing for a short period of time – two to three weeks around the end of April. If the weather is good and the hatch is numerous they can provide splendid sport, especially if there is a stiff breeze.

135

Because of their bulky form and their habit of swarming in a fair breeze many may end up on the water. The trout appear to have a liking for the fly and when available will take them greedily. The fisherman may carry the pattern for season after season and not use it, but if he chances on the right conditions he will curse himself for not having an artificial in his box. The natural fly is all black apart from the grey-white translucent wings. The head and shoulder areas are bulky and the black legs are obvious by their length. Artificials are tied with black floss or herl for the body, and the thorax and head should be emphasized. A rib is added of thread or fine silver wire. The grey wing should be tied flat over the back and a small black cock hackle tied in front of the wing. A main feature is the last two long trailing legs and these can be tied from black pheasant tail fibres knotted in the middle to form knee joints. The artificial should be cast and left to drift over the fish with the aid of the wind.

Miscellaneous (Plate K)

Shows only some of the many and varied creatures that come under the title 'Miscellaneous'. Some are aquatic and some terrestrial. They will all appear at some time in the trout's diet. I do not intend to go into all their life-cycles or into how to fish them, some being more important than others. The Daddy-Long-Legs, for instance, can be a very useful pattern as can the Beetle. I have seen and caught fish that were selectively feeding on one form of terrestrial insect to the exclusion of all else.

One of my fishing friends, Jack Shardlow, caught a large brown trout that was absolutely full of Greenfly. I, myself, fishing under some trees on the River Wharfe, managed, after many attempts, to catch a trout that was avidly taking what I thought to be surface fly. When the fish was examined it contained nothing but dozens of green caterpillars. On certain rivers, and at certain times, terrestrials are a very important part of the trout's food.

The same rules apply to terrestrials that apply to the more 'important' classes of flies. The naturals are there to be used as a pattern. Use them and take into account movement and where the natural is likely to be found, the time of year and at what stage the living insect is being taken.

Plate K. Miscellaneous Flies and Fauna
surface and sub-surface stages (naturals, floating and weighted artificials)

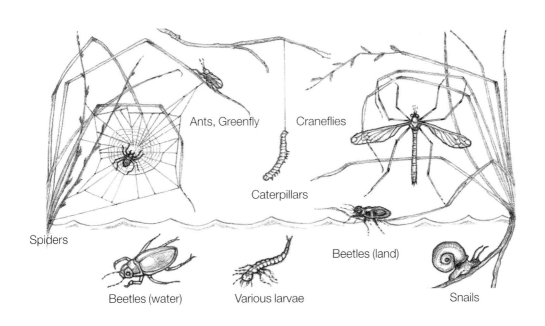

Ants, Greenfly

Craneflies

Caterpillars

Spiders

Beetles (land)

Beetles (water)

Various larvae

Snails

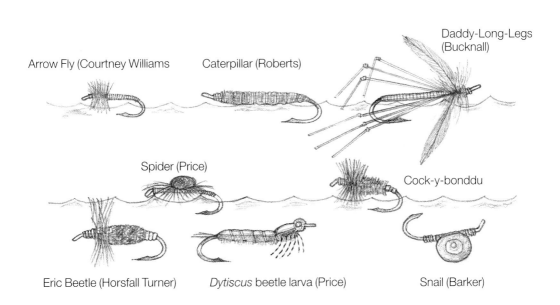

Arrow Fly (Courtney Williams

Caterpillar (Roberts)

Daddy-Long-Legs
(Bucknall)

Spider (Price)

Cock-y-bonddu

Eric Beetle (Horsfall Turner)

Dytiscus beetle larva (Price)

Snail (Barker)

Appendices

Quick Identification

*Numbers in parentheses indicate page number.   * Indicates not illustrated.*

Wings

2 Wings	Flat over body when at rest – go to A	*Diptera*
	Upwinged, dull – go to E	*Ephemeroptera*
	Upwinged, shiny – go to F	*Ephemeroptera*
4 Wings	Flat over body when at rest – go to C	Stoneflies
	Roof-shaped, dull/fine hairs all over – go to D	Sedge Flies
	Roof-shaped, shiny – go to B	Alder
	Upwinged, dull – go to G	*Ephemeroptera*
	Upwinged, shiny – go to H	*Ephemeroptera*

A Diptera   (Several thousand species) (various sizes)
includes   Black Gnats (113)
      Chironomids (19)
      Hawthorn Flies (113)
      Reed Smuts (105)

B Alder   (18mm) (13)

C Stoneflies: Large: (18–24mm)
      Perla Bipunctata   )
      Dinocras cephalotes   )Large Stonefly (42)
      Perlodes microcephala   )
      Medium: (8–14mm)
      Medium Stonefly (*)
      Yellow Sally (45)
      February Red (49)
      Willow Fly (*)
      Small: (5–9mm)
      Early Brown (*)
      Small Brown (45)
      Small Yellow Sally (45)
      Needle Fly (45)

D Sedge-Fly   Large: (13–27mm)
      Great Red Sedge (19)
      Caperer (39)
      Large Cinnamon Sedge (*)
      Silver or Grey Sedge (35)
      Medium: (9–16mm)
      Brown Sedge (35)
      Cinnamon (29)
      Welshman's Button (39)
      Marbled Sedge (32)
            Black Sedge (*)
            Grey Flag (39)
            Yellow Spotted Sedge (29)
            Medium Sedge (*)
            Sand Fly (32)
            Grannom (29)
            Small: (5–10mm)
            Brown Silverhorns (35)
            Black Silverhorns (*)
            Grouse Wing (*)
            Small Red Sedge (32)
            Small Yellow Sedge (*)

E Upwinged Dull: (2 Tails)
      Pond Olive (97)
      Lake Olive (*)

	Pale Evening Dun (89)
	(3 Tails)
	Caenis (Broadwings) (74)
F Upwinged Shiny :	(2 Tails)
	Pond Olive Spinner (97)
	Lake Olive Spinner (*)
	Pale Evening Spinner (89)
	(3 Tails)
	Broadwing (*Caenis*) Spinners (74)
G Upwinged Dull:	(2 Tails) (Small oval or narrow spur-shaped hindwing)
	Large Dark Olive (81)
	Dark Olive (85)
	Medium Olive (81)
	Small Dark Olive (71)
	Pale Watery (71)
	Small Spurwing (89)
	Large Spurwing (89)
	(2 Tails) (Upright hindwings)
	March Brown (101)
	Olive Upright (97)
	Dusky Yellowstreak (93)
	Autumn Dun (74)
	Large Brook Dun (97)
	Large Green Dun (85)
	Late March Brown (101)
	(3 Tails)
	Mayfly (8 & 9)
	Blue Winged Olive (74)
	Turkey Brown (85)
	Purple Dun (101)
	Claret Dun (93)
	Sepia Dun (93)
	Yellow Evening Dun (71)
H Upwinged Shiny:	(2 Tails) (Small oval or narrow spur-shaped hindwing)
	Large Dark Olive Spinner (81)
	Dark Olive Spinner (85)
	Iron Blue Spinner (81)
	Medium Olive Spinner (81)
	Small Dark Olive Spinner (71)
	Little Amber Spinner (Small Spurwing) (89)
	Large Amber Spinner (Large Spurwing) (89)
	Pale Watery Spinner (71)
	(2 Tails) (Upright hindwings)
	March Brown Spinner (101)
	Yellow Upright (97) (Olive Upright)
	Dusky Yellowstreak Spinner (93)
	Autumn Spinner (74)
	Large Brook Spinner (97)
	Large Green Spinner (85)
	Great Red Spinner (Late March Brown) (101)
	(3 Tails)
	Spent Gnat (Mayfly) (8 & 9)
	Sherry Spinner (Blue Winged Olive) (74)
	Turkey Brown Spinner (85)
	Purple Spinner (101)
	Claret Spinner (93)
	Sepia Spinner (93)
	Yellow Evening Spinner (71)

Characteristics of Egg Laying/ Emergence of Adult/Swarming of Ephemeroptera

	Egg Laying	Emergence	Areas used for Swarming
Small Dark Olive	Female goes underwater to lay	Surface of water	Away from the water
Baetis scambus			
Large Dark Olive	Female goes underwater to lay	Surface of water	Away from the water
Baetis rhodani			
Large Brook Dun	Female flies over surface and eggs released in batches	Fully or partly out of water	Over water surface
Ecdyonurus torrentis			
March Brown	Female flies over surface and eggs released in batches	Surface of water	Over water surface
Rhithrogena germanica			
Iron Blue	Female flies over surface and eggs released in batches	Surface of water	Away from the water
Baetis niger/muticus			
Sepia Dun	Female flies over surface and eggs released in batches	Surface of water	Away from the water
Leptophlebia marginata			
Claret Dun	Female flies over surface and eggs released in batches	Surface of water/fully or partly out of water	Away from the water
Leptophlebia vespertina			
Late March Brown	Female flies over surface and eggs released in batches	Surface of water/fully or partly out of water	Over water surface
Ecdyonurus venosus			
Caenis	Female flies over surface and eggs released in batches	Surface of water	Over bankside area
Various			
Blue Winged Olive	Female flies over surface and eggs released in one mass	Surface of water	Away from the water
Ephemerella ignita			
Medium Olive	Female goes underwater to lay	Surface of water	Away from the water
Baetis Vernus			
Turkey Brown	Female flies over surface and eggs released in one mass	Fully or partly out of water	Away from the water
Paraleptophlebia submarginata			
Pale Evening Dun	Female flies over surface and eggs released in batches	Surface of water	Away from the water
Procloeon bifidum			
Olive Upright	Female flies over surface and eggs released in batches	Surface of water	Over water surface
Rithrogena semicolorata			
Small Spurwing	Female flies over surface and eggs released in one mass	Surface of water	Over water surface
Centroptilum luteolum			
Large Spurwing	Female flies over surface and eggs released in one mass	Surface of water	Over water surface
Centroptilum pennulatum			
Yellow Evening Dun	Female flies over surface and eggs released in one mass	Surface of water	Away from the water
Ephemerella notata			
Large Green Dun	Female flies over surface and eggs released in batches	Fully or partly out of water	Over water surface
Ecdyonurus dispar, insignis			
Purple Dun	Female flies over surface and eggs released in one mass	Fully or partly out of water	Away from the water
Paraleptophlebia cincta			
Pale Watery	Female goes underwater to lay	Surface of water	Away from the water
Baetis fuscatus			

Dark Olive	Female flies over surface and eggs released in batches	Surface of water	Away from the water
Baetis Atrebatinus			
Dusky Yellowstreak	Female flies over surface and eggs released in batches	Beneath surface of water	Over bankside area
Heptogenia lateralis			
Pond Olive	The only British Ovoviviparous species.	Surface of water	Away from the water
Cloeon, dipterum	Eggs hatch on contact with water		
Autumn Dun	Female flies over surface and eggs released in batches	Fully or partly out of water	Over water surface
Ecdyonurus dispar			

Bibliography

Chinery, M., *Insects*,Harper Collins,1994.
Elliott, J. and Humpesch*, British Ephemeroptera,* Freshwater Biological Associations*,*1983.
Elliott, Humpesch and Macan, *Larvae of British Eptemeroptera,* Freshwater Biological Associations, 1988
Engelhardt, W., *Pond-Life,* Burke, 1964
Fitter, R. and Manuel, R., *Freshwater Life*,Collins,1986
Goddard, J., *Trout Fly Recognition*, A & C Black,1983
Hynes, H.B.N.,*British Stoneflies,* Freshwater Biological Associations ,1993
Jardine, C., *Dark Pools,* Crowood Press,1991,
     Fly Fishing,1994,Dorling Kindersley
Price, T.,*Tying and Fishing the Nymph,*Blandford,1995
Roberts, J., *A Guide to River Trout Flies,*Crowood Press,1989,
     New Illustrated Dictionary, Allen and Unwin,1988

Useful Addresses

Associations

The Freshwater Biological Association,
Ambleside, Cumbria
Salmon and Trout Association,
Anglers Co-operative Association

Equipment

Lathkill Tackle,Darley Dale, Matlock, Derbyshire

Sportfish,Winforton, Hereford

Collecting Specimens, etc.

Watkins and Doncaster
(Naturalists)
Cranbrook, Kent

Index